its:
ear on

vard

reet

CPAG promotes action for the relief, directly or indirectly, of poverty among children and families with children. We work to ensure that those on low incomes get their full entitlements to welfare benefits. In our campaigning and information work we seek to improve benefits and policies for low-income families in order to eradicate the injustice of poverty. If you are not already supporting us, please consider making a donation, or ask for details of our membership schemes and publications.

Poverty Publication 111

Published by CPAG
94 White Lion Street, London N1 9PF

ISBN 1 901698 73 4

A CIP record for this book is available from the British Library

Cover and design by Devious Designs 0114 2755634
Typeset by Boldface 020 7833 8868
Printed by Russell Press 0115 9784505

Contents

Acknowledgements

I would like to thank Professor Jane Millar of Bath University who read and commented upon early drafts, and Paula Twigg, Beth Lakhani, Sarah Clarke, David Simmons and Judith Paterson for their welfare rights input. Particular thanks also go to Dr Paul Dornan, CPAG's Policy Officer, for his incisive comments and editing.

Thanks are also due to Alison Key for managing the production of this book and to Paula McDiarmid for proofreading the text.

About the author

Marilyn Howard is an independent social policy analyst and is also currently working for the Disability Rights Commission. She has undertaken research and consultancy for voluntary sector organisations, think-tanks and universities, including government-commissioned evaluation. Marilyn is also a member of two government advisory committees on disability. She has advised parliamentary select committees and was a researcher for Alan Howarth CBE MP. A qualified social worker with a law degree and MPhil in social policy, Marilyn has worked as a probation officer, welfare rights adviser and community social worker.

Abbreviations

AHC	After housing costs
BHC	Before housing costs
CTB	Council tax benefit
CTC	Child tax credit
FC	Family credit
HB	Housing benefit
HBAI	Households Below Average Income
IFS	Institute for Fiscal Studies
IS	Income support
JSA	Jobseeker's allowance (income-based)
LCA	Low cost but acceptable
LEA	Local education authority
NAO	National Audit Office
RPI	Retail Prices Index
WFTC	Working families' tax credit
WTC	Working tax credit

Foreword

April 2003 marked the launch of the child tax credit (CTC). The scheme has had its first birthday and now, after a little over a year of operation, is an excellent time for a review of the progress made against its central aim of reducing child poverty.

As an organisation campaigning for the abolition of child poverty, and one with a strong welfare rights focus, CPAG has had mixed views and experiences of the new tax credits. They are a move away from directing additional spending through universal forms of provision, such as child benefit, that CPAG has always supported strongly. Child benefit is simple, well understood, popular and proportionally most valuable to those on the lowest incomes. It remains critical to the incomes of families in general and poorest families in particular. Yet substantial increases in the value of child benefit, and the cost this implies, appear to be off the political map at the moment. Instead, we have 'progressive universalism': all (or most) get something, but the poorest get the most. The principle behind progressive universalism seems to be that policy works most effectively if it universal, but that resource restrictions require the focusing of (limited) resources on the poorest.

The pragmatic test of progressive universalism is its effectiveness in delivery per se, and particularly in delivering most to those on the lowest incomes and in a way appropriate to their circumstances. The analysis in this book shows a rather mixed picture on that front. Child poverty has fallen both on income, and indeed on more material, measures, as a direct result of government policy leading up to and including CTC. We will have to wait to examine take-up rates in detail, but certainly the caseload for CTC appears high. There are, nevertheless, serious structural issues and problems of complexity with CTC, and these appear to bear most heavily on those on the lowest incomes. Where structure and delivery cause hardship, and the evidence in this book shows that they have done, this runs directly counter to the child poverty reduction agenda propounded by the Government.

The structural position, from which many of the problems detailed in this book flow, is the alignment of tax credits with the taxation system and, in particular, the annualised system of assessment. Within an annualised system of assessment there is an inherent potential for individuals to build up large over- and underpayments. An annual system also struggles to fit with weekly assessed benefits, such as income support and housing benefit, causing further problems for poorer families who are more likely to rely on them. This raises the question of the appropriateness of an annual system for CTC (particularly for those on the lowest incomes). For an annual assessment to be retained, it must find a way to meet the needs of the poorest families. The Inland Revenue must minimise both under- and overpayments and, where overpayments occur, exercise proper discretion when deciding whether to recover, and apply reasonable recovery rates and methods. Evidence in the book shows that the way in which overpayments have been clawed back by the Inland Revenue has been ill thought through and unclear, often placing families in genuine hardship.

Much has been made of the problems of the implementation of the tax credit scheme and it is not our intention to re-visit these debates here. Marilyn Howard looks beyond this to examine the longer-term structural and delivery issues. Nevertheless, the problems of the first year of operation have a continued relevance: past administrative errors may cause present-day hardship, and high-profile administrative chaos and maltreatment of recipients by the Inland Revenue may have damaged the reputation of the tax credits scheme. With both of these in mind, CPAG is calling for an amnesty on all overpayments (except those caused by recipient fraud) arising from the first year of operation. Such an amnesty would wipe the slate clean after the early teething troubles and would help the Inland Revenue establish itself as an organisation capable of understanding the hardship that its own administrative practice may cause for lower-income families.

The report card Marilyn Howard has produced gives a mixed picture of progress. What remains clear through all of this is that CTC is central to the Government's ambition of reducing child poverty. For tax credits to help achieve this objective, there must be further investment and they must be administered in a way that effectively protects families from poverty. If administrative problems continue to place families in hardship, tax credits will not be able to make this claim

Paul Dornan

Introduction

Since the Prime Minister's historic pledge in 1999 to end child poverty, many initiatives have been aimed at boosting incomes and services for low-income families. These include the minimum wage, tax credits and the Sure Start programme for children aged under four. In the last 30 years the UK has been at the bottom of the league for child poverty in developed countries,[1] though since 1999 it has moved up by five places. This represents progress, but much more needs to be done to place the UK at the top of the European Union league.

The new tax credits will be a major instrument in further reducing child income poverty and enabling the Government to meet its historic targets. Introduced in April 2003, they represent a major policy change – perhaps the most significant in the last 50 years. Some key changes involve separating out payments for children from those of adults and moving towards an annual (rather than weekly) assessment of income for all families.

The focus of the book

This publication is mainly focussed on the child tax credit (CTC), though in describing how this works it is also necessary to refer to the working tax credit because of the interaction between them.

The book also examines the role of CTC as one of the major mechanisms for tackling income poverty. Current government targets include eradicating child poverty by 2020, halving it by 2010 and reducing it by a quarter in 2004.

The target for 2004 is to be measured by the numbers of children in households with equivalised incomes below 60 per cent of the median, relative to 1998/99. It is measured before housing costs (BHC) or after housing costs (AHC).[2] Child income poverty has reduced by 600,000 (BHC) and 700,000 (AHC) since 1996/97.[3]

With the introduction of CTC and the additional spending for 2004/05, not reflected in the latest figures, the Government looks likely to meet the 2004 target.[4] The yardstick by which the longer-term targets will be measured includes a combination of absolute and relative low-income measures and material deprivation (see Chapter 2).[5] Further reforms needed to meet the long-term poverty targets have been considered in government reviews of child poverty and childcare.

However, as this book will show, there are aspects of the design and delivery of tax credits that could militate against reducing child poverty (for example, the policy and practice of recovering overpayments).

CPAG was concerned to examine the broader issues after one year of the new system of tax credits, with a longer-term emphasis on design and delivery in the future. There have been considerable and well-publicised concerns about the implementation of the new tax credits in 2003.[6] These have included computer failure during the early months of the new system, backlogs and delays in making payments, and an inability to reconcile payments with the amounts authorised.[7] The negative impact on the image of the Inland Revenue and tax credits could have a knock-on impact on public confidence and take-up.[8] This book does not dwell on these implementation problems *per se* as the focus is on longer-term changes. However, the experience of some families during 2003/04 highlights the need for further reform.

Inevitably, CPAG's welfare rights interest has focused on areas of the new tax credits where the system has not been working well and, whilst not detracting from the role of CTC in increasing incomes for the poorest families with children, there remain some design features of tax credits that need further modification for its poverty-reducing role to be maximized.

This book covers some of the detail of tax credit rules (such as overpayments) in order to highlight areas where the design of the new system could be improved. However, it is not a technical guide. For an authoritative statement of the law, readers should refer to CPAG's *Welfare Benefits and Tax Credits Handbook* and regular *Welfare Rights Bulletins*. This book draws on existing literature on tax credits and includes some case studies from CPAG's monitoring network on tax credits, which gathered case evidence from advisers across the UK. Each chapter also includes policy recommendations for the longer term.

Structure of the book

The book begins with an outline of the tax credits and the reasons for introducing them (Chapter 1). Then the structure of CTC is examined, together with a review of the potential adequacy of payments in meeting need and in reducing child income poverty (Chapter 2).

A major change introduced by tax credits, the annual assessment of income, is described in the next chapter, including the impact of rules for reporting changes in circumstances (Chapter 3). This is followed by an examination of what happens when people are paid too much, and the implications of having a tax credit overpayment, in particular for child income poverty (Chapter 4). The next chapter discusses what happens when people are paid too little, and the importance of quality of service and take-up of entitlement in reducing child income poverty (Chapter 5).

Then the book reviews the interrelationships between the new tax credits and other benefits like housing benefit and 'passported' benefits or services such as free school meals (Chapter 6). The next chapter considers childcare and the childcare tax credit and their role in reducing child poverty (Chapter 7). In the final chapter issues for the future are examined, together with a summary of main points from each chapter and key recommendations for the future.

Notes

1 L Harker and others, *Poverty in a Land of Plenty Five Years On*, End Child Poverty Coalition, 2004

2 See M Brewer, *What do the Child Poverty Targets Mean for the Child Tax Credit? An update*, Briefing Note 41, Institute for Fiscal Studies, 2003

3 Department for Work and Pensions, *Households Below Average Income 1994/95–2002/03*, 2004

4 M Brewer and others, *Poverty and Inequality in Britain*, Institute for Fiscal Studies, 2004

5 Department for Work and Pensions, *Measuring Child Poverty*, 2003

6 See for example, Evidence Briefing, *New Tax Credits: CAB clients' experience of the first two months*, Citizens Advice, 2003

7 House of Commons Committee of Public Accounts, *Inland Revenue: tax credits*, Fourteenth Report of Session 2003/04, HC 89, 2004

8 National Audit Office, *Comptroller and Auditor General's Standard Report on the Accounts of the Inland Revenue 2002/03*, HC 1072, 2003

One

What are tax credits?

This chapter outlines the development of financial support for families with children, from child benefit and the early in-work benefits to the 2003 tax credits. The objectives of tax credits are discussed. In particular it addresses the separation of child payments from those payable to adults, making child payments more 'visible', and the concept of 'progressive universalism' (where all families gain but the poorest gain most). The main features of tax credits are described, including examples of how tax credits are calculated.

A brief history of tax credits for families with children

Payments for children have been made in several ways: through 'universal'[1] child benefit; as increases to benefits payable to adults in the family; and as tax allowances. The abolition of the married couple's tax allowance funded increases in the income support (IS) rates for children under age 11 and a 'children's tax credit', in 2001. The children's tax credit reduced liability against income tax and was intended to be an interim measure pending the implementation of the new tax credits.

In-work support for families with children was originally introduced in 1971 as a means-tested benefit for people working more than 30 hours a week (family income supplement). Subsequently this was replaced by family credit (FC), the working hours for eligibility were progressively reduced and a disregard for childcare costs added. Alongside the introduction of the national minimum wage in 1999, the working families' tax credit (WFTC) replaced FC. It was intended to reduce the stigma attached to claiming benefit, encourage higher take-up and demonstrate the rewards of working. Compared with its predecessor, WFTC was more generous in the treatment of childcare costs, was payable to people higher up the income scale, administered by the Inland Revenue and payable via the employer for many claimants.

Why were the new tax credits introduced?

In Budget 2000 the Government announced its intention to create a new generation of tax credits, separating support for children from support for adults by creating a child tax credit (CTC) and a working tax credit (WTC). The main goals of CTC are to support families and reduce child income poverty. The new tax credits were also considered integral to the Government's aims to make work pay, and to create simpler and 'lighter touch' means-testing. A further aim was to reverse the earlier impact of payment via the employer by paying CTC to the person, usually the mother, who was the main carer of children in the family (whilst retaining payroll payments for WTC).

The objectives of tax credits

In particular, the aims of the new tax credits were as follows.

- **To be portable between benefits and work.** The aim was to make it easier for people to move into work, as CTC can be payable whether or not someone is working (though the amount may change). Families in work can claim either WTC and CTC, or CTC only.

- **To give payments for children to the main carer.** For claims made jointly by a couple, CTC and the childcare element of WTC can be paid to whoever is the 'main carer' of the children, involving a £2 billion transfer of CTC to the main carer.[2] This was intended, in part, to make CTC a more visible payment for children and was based on evidence that payments to the main carer (often the mother) would be most likely to be spent on children (and contribute towards a reduction in child poverty).[3] The 2004 Budget announced an intention in principle to move away from the controversial payments via the employer towards direct payment.[4]

- **To be a more transparent, streamlined system bringing all income-related payments into a single credit.** Rather than having different rates of allowances for children based on the work status of their parents, CTC involves a distinct system of payments for children across work and income status (though actual amounts payable depend on income). Identifying payments as specifically for children was intended to help parents understand their entitlement. However, both CTC and WTC are claimed and paid as one award, and there are some complex interactions between them (such as when overpayments are recovered).

- **To have a common framework for assessment and payment, so all families are included in the same system.** As well as being administered by the Inland Revenue, treatment and definitions of income broadly follow income tax conventions rather than benefits rules. This includes an annual assessment and new rules for dealing with changes in circumstances as well as more stringent rules on overpayments and the introduction of penalties.

An assessment of the extent to which the operation of tax credits in the first year has met these objectives will be discussed in the final chapter.

The objectives of child tax credit

CTC offers both a common means-tested payment for poor families, irrespective of whether or not they are working, and makes it explicit that it expects this payment to meet the needs of children, separate from other means-tested payments meeting general needs of poor families (like IS).[5] One of the dilemmas of the former child additions to benefits was that they aimed to provide for the subsistence needs of children whose parents were out of work, whilst also keeping a gap between wages and benefits to preserve work incentives.[6] The aim is to reduce such confusion by having separate mechanisms for work incentives and for supporting children. One advantage was expected to be greater 'transparency' (in relation to identifying payments specifically for children) so that parents would understand their entitlement and public debate about child support and child poverty would be facilitated.[7] Transparency more generally is discussed in Chapter 3 and in the summary.

Specifically, the objectives of CTC are the following.

- To support all families with children.
- To reduce the stigma attached to claiming, mainly by including 90 per cent of families within the same system and being administered by the Inland Revenue.
- To contribute towards eradicating child income poverty.

Using the same mechanism to achieve both aims is integral to the idea of 'progressive universalism' – ie, most families get something, but the poorest get more. However, there may be some tension between these objectives.

The main features of tax credits

CTC and WTC were introduced in April 2003, with all child elements within IS and jobseeker's allowance (JSA) being brought into CTC during 2004. CTC also extends support to some families with children previously excluded from IS/JSA (students and student nurses).

'Lighter touch' means-testing

The main differences between means-tested benefits like IS and the 2003 tax credits system involve the shift from a weekly means test administered by the Department for Work and Pensions to an annual assessment (described more fully in Chapter 3) more akin to the tax system, administered by the Inland Revenue. The aim was to introduce 'lighter touch' means-testing that would be less intrusive for claimants and easier for administrators.

Calculating tax credits

The amount of tax credits to which someone is entitled depends on family circumstances and income. CTC and WTC consist of different elements (for each child, and per family). Tax credits are calculated by comparing income with one or more of the set amounts (income thresholds), with income above those amounts being reduced by a set percentage ('taper').

The three income thresholds for 2004/05 are:

- £5,060 for people claiming both WTC and CTC;
- £13,480 for people claiming CTC only; *and*
- £50,000 for people claiming the family element only.

Example

How tax credits are calculated

Tracey is a lone parent with two children, aged four and ten. Because she has no earnings and is getting IS, she is entitled to maximum tax credits.

CTC

Family element	£545
Child element	£1,625
Child element	£1,625
Total	**£3,795**

Marsha and Bill live with their two children (aged four and ten). Their only income is Bill's full-time earnings of £19,146 (plus child benefit, but this is ignored in the tax credits calculation).

Their maximum WTC and CTC entitlement is:

WTC

Basic element	£1,570
Couple element	£1,545
30-hour element	£640
Total	**£3,755**

CTC

Family element	£545
Child element	£1,625
Child element	£1,625
Total	**£3,795**

Total maximum = £7,550

The relevant threshold for Marsha and Bill (because they are claiming WTC and CTC) is £5,060.

Their income (£19,146) minus the threshold (£5,060) is £14,086 (the 'excess income').

37 per cent of the excess income = £5,211

Deduct this from the maximum of both tax credits
£7,550 – £5,211= £2,339

People receiving IS/JSA should be awarded the maximum tax credit; those with incomes above the first threshold have their award of WTC and CTC gradually reduced at 37p in the £, and by £1 in every £15 of gross earnings above the income threshold of £50,000.

Tax credits are assessed on gross income (rather than net of deductions), entailing a lower withdrawal rate (37 per cent) to make it equivalent to the (higher) taper applying to net earnings for the former WFTC (55 per cent).[8] Tapers can affect 'marginal deduction rates' – ie, the rate at which each additional £ is lost through higher tax/national insurance deductions and withdrawal of benefits and tax credits.

Example

Marginal deduction rate calculation

Income tax can reduce £1 of earnings by 22 pence, national insurance deductions by 11 pence, WTC by 37 pence. This gives a marginal deduction rate of 70 per cent (ie, for every £1 earned 70 pence is withdrawn in tax and tax credits).[9]

This can be further reduced by 65 pence for housing benefit and 20 pence for council tax benefit for every £1 of take-home pay less WTC (adding 25.5 per cent to the deductions above, leading to marginal tax rates of 95.5 per cent – ie, a deduction of almost 96 pence for every £1).

The change from net to gross income could improve incentives for a second earner in a couple by reducing the marginal deduction rates, because if a second earner worked for wages low enough not to attract tax or national insurance contributions, their marginal deduction rate would be better under a gross, rather than net, income taper.[10] As a result of in-work reforms, marginal deduction rates have reduced since 1997, with nearly half a million fewer people facing deductions of 70 per cent.[11] However, more are facing marginal deduction rates of 60-70 per cent because tax credits extend further up the income scale to give more help to more families (see Table 1.1).

Table 1.1

The effect of government reforms on marginal deduction rates: numbers of working households*

	Before Budget 1998	2004/05 system
Over 100%	5,000	0
Over 90%	130,000	40,000
Over 80%	300,000	190,000
Over 70%	740,000	265,000
Over 60%	760,000	1,700,000

Source: *Budget 2004*, p97

* Where at least one person works 16 hours a week

Where incomes are over the threshold, credits are withdrawn in the following order:

- WTC (excluding the childcare element);
- WTC childcare element;
- CTC (excluding the family element);
- CTC family element.

The impact of tax credits

In April 2004, 30 per cent of families with children had incomes below the £13,480 threshold and 85 per cent were on incomes below £50,000.[12] The tax credits translate into different levels of support for families depending on their income (see Figure 1.1).

About six million families were expected to fall within the reach of tax credits and by the end of the first year there were indeed six million tax credit recipients: 1.4 million where no adult was in work; 1.59 million receiving maximum CTC and WTC; and 1.89 families in work receiving the family element only.[13] This does not necessarily imply full take-up, as this would suggest that the initial projections were wholly correct – which we do not yet know (see Chapter 5).

We will now turn to CTC and its contribution to reducing child income poverty in more detail.

Figure 1.1

Levels of support for families, April 2004

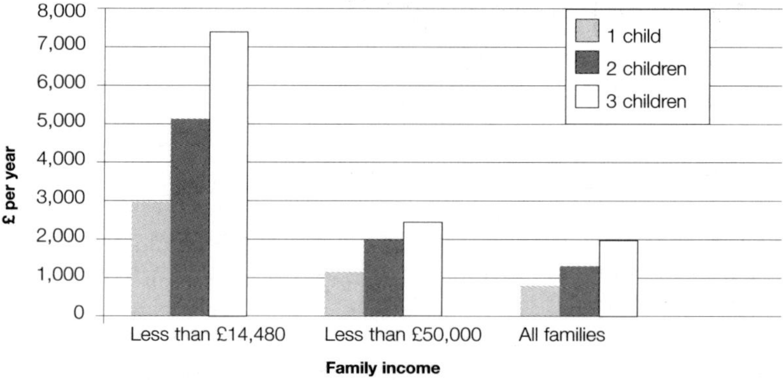

Source: HM Treasury, *Budget 2004*, HC301, 2004, p102

Notes

1 Those 'subject to immigration control' are excluded from child benefit entitlement.

2 HM Treasury, *Pre-Budget Report*, Cm 6042, 2003

3 Department for Work and Pensions, *Opportunity For All*, Cm 5956, 2003

4 HM Treasury, *Budget 2004*, HC301, 2004

5 D Hirsch, *A Credit to Children: the UK's radical reform of children's benefits in an international perspective*, Joseph Rowntree Foundation, 2000

6 See J Brown, *The Future of Family Income Support*, Policy Studies Institute, 1987, p13

7 HM Treasury, *The Modernisation of Britain's Tax and Benefit System No 6*, 2000

8 *The Tax Credits Bill*, House of Commons Library Research Paper 01/110, 2001

9 Department for Work and Pensions, *Tax Benefit Model Tables April 2003*, 2004, p7

10 M Brewer and others, *Credit where it's due? An assessment of the new tax credits*, Institute for Fiscal Studies Commentary 86, 2001

11 See note 4

12 See note 4

13 Inland Revenue, *Child and Working Tax Credits Quarterly Statistics*, April 2004

Two

Child tax credit and child poverty

Key points in this chapter include a discussion of the role of tax credits in reducing income poverty and raising incomes, as well as the adequacy of the child tax credit (CTC) in meeting the needs of children. A range of policy options for raising the level of financial support for children are then discussed.

The role of tax credits in raising incomes

The former tax credits – working families' tax credit (WFTC) and disabled person's tax credit – and the new generation have raised incomes for many families, and should be recognised as a success for the Government in targeting resources on families with children. Between 1997 and 2003, financial support for children rose by £9.2 billion in real terms, an increase of 64 per cent. By October 2004, the Government estimates that:

- families with children should be, on average, £1,350 a year better off, with the poorest families £3,000 better off;
- a single-earner family on half average earnings with two young children should be £3,790 a year better off.[1]

Between 1999 and 2001, average weekly incomes for couples went up by a third and for lone parents by a quarter, and families who left income support (IS) and received WFTC by 2001 saw their incomes rise by 73 per cent on average.[2] Fewer tax credit recipients experienced hardship, declining from one in five in 1999 to one in twenty in 2002.[3] However, whilst the additional money paid through IS also seems to have reduced rates of severe hardship among out-of-work families, more than one in five workless families, especially lone parents, experienced severe hardship in

2002.[4] This suggests that the target for reducing poverty in the longer term requires further policy measures.

The role of child tax credit in reducing child income poverty

CTC is a major tool in combating child income poverty, and recognises that financial support for children (rather than parental employment) can reduce the numbers of children living below a set poverty line, such as in Australia.[5] The Institute for Fiscal Studies (IFS) estimates that CTC is likely to amount to half of the income of households with children in poverty in 2004, the rest comprising other means-tested benefits and tax credits, maintenance and net earnings.[6] However, if any of the other sources grow more slowly than median incomes, CTC will need to grow faster to ensure that child income poverty targets are met.

In 2002/03, 200,000 children were taken out of income poverty over the previous year, with 600,000 fewer before housing costs (BHC) and 700,000 fewer after housing costs (AHC) since 1996/97 (see Table 2.1 below).[7] This represents a reduction of 16 per cent (BHC) and 14 per cent (AHC), leaving the Government having to achieve another 8-10 per cent to meet the 2004 target. The indications are that whilst numbers have fallen, there are people a long way below the poverty line (such as those experiencing severe hardship for prolonged periods – figures on the numbers below half the median are included alongside those for 60 per cent in the table to demonstrate this) and so their situation remains to be improved.

The Government proposes to change the way it assesses progress on reducing poverty in the longer term, which will include measures of absolute low income, relative low income and material deprivation.[8] Child poverty would be deemed to fall when all three indicators are dropping (though it is unclear if halving child poverty means halving on all, or some, indicators). Changes to 'equivalisation' (the weighting given to certain family types) will also give greater weight to the needs of younger children and lone-parent households. The relative low-income measure would be the same as now but only on a BHC basis, not taking account of the effect of housing costs. Some 900,000 fewer children are likely to be 'poor' on this measure, mainly in households with higher housing costs, living in the south and east of England.[9] CPAG has expressed concern that this alter-

Table 2.1

Children taken out of income poverty

	50% median 2002/03		**60% median 2002/03**	
	BHC	**AHC**	**BHC**	**AHC**
Millions and per cent of children below the threshold	1.3 m (10%)	2.4 m (19%)	2.6 m (21%)	3.6 m (28%)
Numbers taken out of poverty since 1996/97	–0.3m	–0.6m	–0.6m	–0.7m

Source: Department for Work and Pensions, *Households Below Average Income 1994/95–2002/03*, 2004

ation could reduce the number of children defined as poor because of changes to the yardsticks used to measure poverty and not the effectiveness of policies to tackle child poverty.[10]

To be consistent with the lowest relative poverty rates in Europe, the target to eradicate poverty by 2020 would probably need to reduce the relative low-income rate to 5–10 per cent. It is also an apparent Department for Work and Pensions objective to reduce the material deprivation rate to zero.[11] Meeting the longer-term poverty target could be more challenging since it involves helping the most disadvantaged.

Arrangements for uprating

The different elements of CTC offer a range of mechanisms for uprating. The elements (see Table 2.2) consist of:

- a family element of £545 a year for all families with incomes up to £58,000 a year;
- a child element of £1,625 a year for each child in low-income families;
- a higher family element for families with a baby;
- extra credits for families with a disabled child.

The Government has promised to increase the per child element of CTC in line with average earnings until the end of this Parliament. The per child element increased in April 2004 by £180 a year (or £3.50 a week), £130 above average earnings growth. The thresholds and rates for each element are in Table 2.2 below.

Table 2.2

Working tax credit and child tax credit annual amounts in cash terms, 2003 and 2004

	2003/04	2004/05	Change in cash terms
Working tax credit elements			
Basic	1,525	1,570	(+45)
Couple and lone parent	1,500	1,545	(+45)
30-hour	620	640	(+20)
Disability	2,040	2,100	(+60)
Severe disability	865	890	(+25)
Childcare element			
Maximum eligible cost, 1 child	135 pw	135 pw	–
Maximum eligible cost, 2+ child	200 pw	200 pw	–
% eligible costs covered	70	70	–
50+ return to work 16–29 hours	1,045	1,075	(+30)
50+ return to work 30+ hours	1,565	1,610	(+45)
Child tax credit elements			
Family	545	545	–
Baby addition to family	545	545	–
Child	1,445	1,625	(+180)
Disability	2,155	2,215	(+60)
Severe disability	865	890	(+25)
Income thresholds and tapers			
First income threshold	5,060	5,060	–
First taper (%)	37	37	–
Second income threshold	50,000	50,000	–
Second taper (%)	6.67	6.67	–
First threshold for those entitled to child tax credit only	13,230	13,480	(+250)

Source: *Pre-Budget Report*, Cm 6042, December 2003

As can be seen from Table 2.2, the thresholds and family element were fixed at their April 2003 levels. The real value of the family element will be £15.26 a year lower in 2004/05 than in the previous year.[12] The IFS also estimates that:[13]

- freezing the thresholds and CTC family element will *increase* child income poverty by around 25,000 in 2004/05 (compared with what it would have been had the tax credit elements risen with inflation);
- tax credit changes overall should *reduce* child income poverty by between 160,000 and 210,000 as the per child element increases are targeted on the poorest half of families, but 2.9 million middle and high income families with children lose in real terms.

The assumption for future years, only recently noticed by commentators, is that the thresholds and family element will remain at the April 2003 (cash) levels indefinitely (with only per child elements increasing with average earnings).[14] This arrangement contrasts with social security benefits, required in law to be reviewed annually to determine whether they have retained their value relative to the general level of prices,[15] although there is no requirement actually to uprate income-related benefits. Historically, child benefit has been uprated by the Retail Prices Index (RPI), though it has lost value at certain points in time (see also policy options below).[16]

During the 1980s and 1990s, the UK fell behind other countries as benefit levels failed to rise to match the overall standard of living; in Sweden, two-thirds of families were lifted out of poverty because of state benefits, compared with only a third in the UK.[17] With 'relative' poverty measures, if CTC loses value over time it cannot contribute towards meeting child income poverty targets. Ending child poverty by 2020 will require further efforts to increase the incomes of the poorest.

The role of child tax credit in meeting the needs of children

The separation of payments for children from more general payments to adults means that, in theory, this payment is more explicitly intended to meet the needs of the child (reinforced by payments to the main carer). In practice, it is not easy to separate completely the costs of children from other shared goods, and spending on children can interact with spending on adults (parents often going without to meet their children's needs).

In addition to CTC, the purpose of child benefit has been to contribute towards the extra costs of a child. However, child benefit was meant to be a general contribution rather than meeting all of the costs. Child benefit includes a higher amount for the first child, the rate for second and subsequent children now being 66 per cent of the first.[18] One review of the international evidence suggested that in no country does the state try to provide a universal benefit to cover the *full* cost of children; but some countries, including the UK, now have tools like CTC which aim to cover more of the full cost of raising children for parents on a low income, while paying less to those on middle and higher incomes.[19]

In 2001, a House of Commons select committee indicated that there was a case for working towards a maximum award of CTC for families on the lowest incomes to reflect what parents need to spend on their children.[20] Likewise, one of CPAG's principles is for a 'minimum income standard' for children sufficiently adequate to avoid poverty.

In 2002/03, the poverty line (60 per cent of median incomes) for a family with two children aged 5 and 11 was £283 (for a couple) and £207 (for a lone parent).[21] This is similar to the Family Budget Unit figures for the 'low cost but acceptable' (LCA) budget (though it should be noted that this budget represents a minimum – set at a very stringent level – below which health, child development and social inclusion are at risk). The LCA budget for 2003 (excluding alcohol and childcare costs) was:

- £237 a week for a couple, local authority tenants, with a boy aged 10 and a girl aged 4, no earner;
- £199 a week for a lone parent, also a local authority tenant, with a boy aged 10 and a girl aged 4, not an earner.[22]

The rate per child (£1,625 a year, or £31.25 a week) was originally set at a level to be more generous than IS/JSA child allowances.[23] While this represents significant gains it may not be meeting all of the costs of children in poorer families. For example, as we will see in Chapter 4, reduced payments resulting from the recovery of overpayments can mean that people are living on incomes below this level. Furthermore, whether CTC can meet the needs of children in the poorest families depends on tax credits being claimed by those on low incomes who are eligible (see Chapter 5).

Policy options for increasing financial support for

children

The current structure of financial support for families with children means that the Government has three main ways to increase their incomes.

- **Child benefit**, also administered by the Inland Revenue, which helps all families with children regardless of income.
- The **family element** of CTC, which directs money to all but the richest 10 per cent of families.
- The **per child element** of CTC, which directs money to the poorest half of families.[24]

Child benefit increases

As a payment that is almost 'universal' in reaching most families with children, take-up of child benefit is high.[25] Over seven million families are receiving child benefit for almost 13 million children.[26] Low-income families can receive both child benefit and CTC, and child benefit is not taken into account as income for tax credit purposes.[27] The current child benefit rate is £16.50 a week for the first child and £11.05 for subsequent children. Child benefit has not been increased in real terms since 1999. Consequently, there are fears that it may further reduce in value over time, relative to living standards. Benefits like child benefit are expensive and many countries have moved away from such an approach, though countries with low poverty rates tend to have generous flat rate allowances with higher rates of personal taxation. Notwithstanding these differences, the Work and Pensions Committee recommended that there should be a commitment to retain and up-rate child benefit to enhance its real value.[28]

As it goes to most families, the contribution of child benefit on its own to reducing child income poverty when there is considerable inequality in the distribution of incomes looks less favourable than the income-related CTC. When considering the 2004 child income poverty target, the IFS has suggested that:

- a £3 a week increase in child benefit from April 2004 could lift around 200,000 children out of poverty at a cost of £2 billion; *while*

Figure 2.1
Gainers from child benefit and child tax credit increases

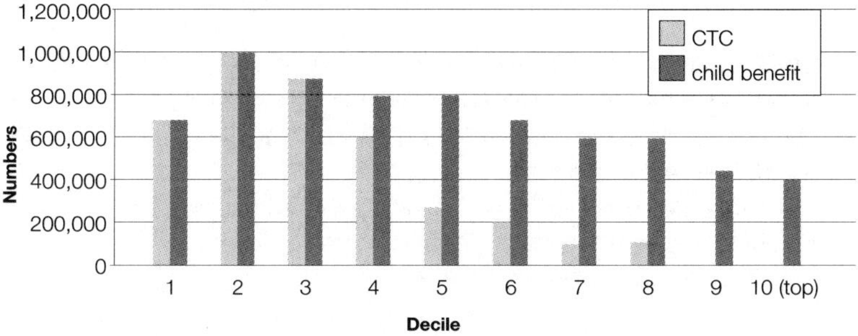

Source: House of Commons *Hansard*, 19 April 2004, col 21w

Note: There are more families with children in the second decile

- the £3.50 increase in the CTC per child element lifted 160,000 children out of poverty at a cost of £885 million.[29]

Increasing child benefit by £260 a year (£5 a week) could cost £3.4 billion, and £545 a year (£10.48 a week) could cost £7.1 billion.[30] Figure 2.1 compares child benefit with CTC increases by income deciles (tenths), showing the gains across the income distribution.

Child tax credit increases

The IFS has modelled several CTC options (costing the same amount), which have different effects on family types and on the numbers of children taken out of income poverty.[31]

Child element increases

Increasing the per child element is more effective in distributing resources to low-income and larger families.

- The IFS estimates that increasing the child element by £3 a week would lift 240,000 children out of income poverty; a £5 increase would lift 395,000 children out of income poverty.

- Increasing the per child element by £545 a year (£10.48 a week) could reduce the number of children living in households with incomes below 60 per cent of the median (AHC) by around one million.[32]

Estimates by Holly Sutherland for the House of Commons Work and Pensions Committee suggested that, other trends remaining constant, the extra income needed to halve poverty by 2010 would, at 2004 prices, be approximately:

- £5 per child per week (on a BHC basis); *and*
- £10 per child per week (on an AHC basis).[33]

Large families

Almost half (45 per cent) of children in income poverty live in families with more than three children and compared with smaller families they are more likely to have a younger child, to be from Pakistani, Indian or Bangladeshi communities, to be out of work and to be in hardship. Similar proportions of lone parents and couples have three or more children, but more families are headed by two parents than one, so large families tend to contain two adults.[34] Hence, one policy option is to target help to large families and this has been recommended by the Work and Pensions Committee.[35] This could be achieved in two ways.

- Introducing an additional payment per family. The IFS modelled a 'large family premium' of £845 a year payable to those with more than three children with joint incomes of below £50,000. This would raise 210,000 children out of income poverty at a cost of about £1 billion, though the richer half of large families would gain more than the poorer.[36]
- Increasing the per child element for larger families. For example, an increase of £1,625 a year to the per child element for fourth and subsequent children would help 320,000 households at an estimated cost of £0.7 billion, reducing the number of children living in households with below 60 per cent median incomes (AHC) by 300,000.[37] Gainers would be in the bottom six deciles, most (120,000) being in the second decile.

Younger children

The 'baby tax credit' increases the family element where there is a child under one in the family. MPs have recommended that there should be no age-related element in the per child element though the Government has made an exception for babies because of the evidence of acute need at that time.[38] One question is whether families with a child under five could be targeted for additional support (helping families that are more likely to have younger children, such as lone parents and larger families). There is some evidence that having a child under five is associated with being less likely to move out of hardship – for lone parents at least.[39] Increasing the per child element of CTC by £545 a year for children under five would help two million households at an estimated cost of £0.5 billion, reducing the number of children living in households with below 60 per cent median incomes (AHC) by 200,000.[40] The numbers gaining, by income decile, are shown in Table 2.3 below.

Table 2.3

Households gaining from increasing the per child element for children under five

Income decile	Number of households gaining
1 (bottom)	300,000
2	500,000
3	500,000
4	300,000
5	200,000
6	100,000
7	100,000
8	–
9	–
10 (top)	–
Total	**2,000,000**

Source: House of Commons, *Hansard*, 19 April 2004, col 19w

Notes: – = figures of less than 50,000

There are more households with children in the second decile than the first

Disabled children

The disability element is payable in addition to the child element for any disabled child in the family. Families with one or more disabled children will often face additional expenses because of the child's disability and a lower likelihood of working, compounded by difficulties in finding appropriate childcare.[41] Though the disabled child element was increased in the *Pre-Budget Report*, the rise was less than the increase in the per child element. Further increases could be made in line with average earnings, as per the child element.

Key stage child development credits

Unlike the focus on weekly increases for younger children discussed above, there is also some evidence that a need for 'lumpy' items (like clothing) can occur at older ages (for example, 9 and 14). One option might be to make lump-sum payments ('child development credits') at the key stages in a child's life that correspond to times of need for such lumpy items.[42] The Work and Pensions Committee also recommended that lump-sum payments could be made at key stages during the lives of children in severe and persistent poverty.[43] This could be particularly important as a means of meeting longer-term child poverty targets.

Future policy options

- Maintaining and improving the value of child benefit as the bedrock of support for most families with children.
- Ensuring that CTC continues to contribute towards reducing child income poverty by uprating the per child element so that it is regularly above earnings by substantial amounts.
- Considering ways to target additional help to poorer families with more than three children and where there is a child under five.
- Uprating the disabled child element to match the child element rises.
- Exploring the feasibility of making additional lump-sum 'child development credits' to children at key stages as a contribution towards meeting longer-term child poverty targets.

Notes

1 HM Treasury, *Budget 2004*, HC 301, 2004
2 S Vegeris and J Perry, *Families and Children 2001: living standards and the children*, Department for Work and Pensions Research Report 190, 2003
3 A Marsh and S Vegeris, 'Employment and Child Poverty', in P Dornan (ed), *Ending Child Poverty by 2020: the first five years*, Child Poverty Action Group, 2004
4 See note 3
5 D Hirsch, *A Credit to Children: the UK's radical reform of children's benefits in an international perspective*, Joseph Rowntree Foundation, 2000
6 M Brewer, *What do the Child Poverty Targets Mean for the Child Tax Credit? An update*, Institute for Fiscal Studies Briefing Note 41, 2003
7 Department for Work and Pensions, *Households Below Average Income 1994/95–2002/03*, 2004
8 See Department for Work and Pensions, *Measuring Child Poverty*, 2003
9 M Brewer and others, *Poverty and Inequality in Britain*, Institute for Fiscal Studies, 2004
10 See for example, P Dornan, 'Defining Income Poverty out of Existence?' *Poverty 117*, pp12–16, Child Poverty Action Group, 2004
11 See note 8, p20
12 HM Treasury, *Supplementary Note to the Department for Work and Pensions Select Committee Inquiry into Child Poverty*, Volume III, 2004
13 M Brewer, *Will the Government Hit its Child Poverty Target in 2004/05?*, Institute for Fiscal Studies Briefing Note 47, 2004
14 *Budget 2003*, p203 and M Brewer, *Will the Government Hit its Child Poverty Target in 2004/05?*, Institute for Fiscal Studies Briefing Note 47, 2004, footnote 4
15 s150 Social Security Administration Act 1992
16 Department for Work and Pensions, *Annual Abstract of Statistics for Benefit Contributions and Indices of Prices and Earnings*, 2003
17 L Harker and others, *Poverty in a Land of Plenty Five Years On*, End Child Poverty Coalition, 2004
18 *The Tax Credits Bill*, House of Commons Library Research Paper 01/110, 2001
19 See note 5
20 Social Security Committee, *Integrated Child Credit*, Second Report of Session 2000/01, HC 72, 2001
21 Measured before housing costs; see Department for Work and Pensions *Households Below Average Income 1994/05–2002/03*, 2004
22 Family Budget Unit, *Families with Children: low cost but acceptable: April 2003* at www.york.ac.uk/res/fbu

23 HM Treasury, *The Modernisation of Britain's Tax and Benefit System No 10*, 2002

24 See note 6

25 Eligibility depends on rules about responsibility for a child and immigration status.

26 Inland Revenue, *Child Benefit Quarterly Statistics*, November 2003

27 *Welfare Benefits and Tax Credits Handbook 2004/05*, Child Poverty Action Group, p1348

28 House of Commons Work and Pensions Committee, *Child Poverty in the UK*, Second Report of Session 2003/04, HC 85-1, 2004

29 See note 28

30 House of Commons *Hansard*, 19 April 2004, col 21w

31 See note 6

32 House of Commons *Hansard*, 19 April 2004, col 20w

33 See note 28, para 229

34 Department for Work and Pensions, *Opportunity For All*, Cm 5956, 2003

35 See note 28

36 See note 6

37 House of Commons *Hansard*, 19 April 2004, col 19w

38 See note 20 and government reply

39 See note 2

40 See note 37

41 See for example, P Russell, *Disabled Children, their Families and Child Poverty*, End Child Poverty Campaign and Council for Disabled Children, 2003

42 M Howard, *Lump Sums: roles for the social fund in ending child poverty*, Child Poverty Action Group, Family Welfare Association and National Council for One Parent Families, 2003, p27 lumpy index

43 See note 28

Three

Assessing income and reporting changes

The overall aim of tax credits was to introduce a 'lighter touch' means-testing. To achieve this aim, the tax credits system has an annual assessment of income. This has been a significant change and central to the experiences of claimants in the first year of operation. This chapter first examines the implications of annual, rather than weekly, assessments for low-incomes families, then looks at the impact of the rules for reporting changes in circumstances. A discussion of the balance between responsiveness and simplicity is followed by some policy options for the longer term.

Annual assessments

Before 2003, income was assessed either weekly (as with means-tested benefits like income support) or based on income at the time of claim, payable for a fixed period of six months with awards not revised until the end of that period (working families' tax credit (WFTC)). In contrast, child tax credit (CTC) and working tax credit (WTC) awards are based on *annual* income and run until the end of the financial year. The calculation is based on income received in the tax year before the claim is made and is set to last for a year, though with some provision to take into account changes during the year (for more detail, see Appendix 1). The income test applies to both partners in a couple.

Payments are usually based on the previous year's income, but for the first year of operation (2003/04) tax credit awards were based on income during the tax year 2001/02. By April 2004 almost three-quarters (3.3 million) of working families had awards based on the 2001/02 tax year.[1] So in that first year, income data was two years old, and so problems of under- and overpayments were particularly likely to occur for this group (see Chapter 4).

Because payments are based on assumed income from the previous year decisions are only provisional, with the final decision being based on actual income for the relevant tax year.[2] An *initial* decision is made about whether to award tax credits and at what rate. At the end of the tax year a *final* decision is made on whether someone is entitled to tax credits and by how much, and whether the initial decision was correct. Underpayments are payable to the claimant as a lump sum and overpayments are usually recovered (see Chapter 4).[3]

One of the consequences of this annual approach is that people will only have a degree of certainty about their entitlement after the Inland Revenue has undertaken its end of year reconciliations. End of year reconciliation is also a newer feature of the Australian system. One of the reasons for its introduction was that families with the same *annual* incomes would receive the same family benefit, irrespective of how they chose to receive it.[4] In the first year of this change, more than 12 times as many families were overpaid as under the previous system and media reporting led to the first A$1,000 of overpayments being waived. It appeared that families were more likely to underestimate than overestimate their income, but it is not clear whether this was deliberate or whether family incomes were more variable than expected. Such a system puts a premium on claimants getting the right information at the right time.

There is further potential for confusion as a CTC claim is based on the *previous* year's income but on personal circumstances that apply in the *current year* at the date of claim.

Responding to and reporting changes

The aim of CTC was to provide continuity of support for those not experiencing significant changes in income or circumstances with the ability to adjust quickly for those facing major changes.[5] So although awards will last for up to a year, the amount received can be altered to reflect changes in circumstances, which was intended to be more responsive than WFTC.[6] A claim or adjustment can be backdated (or take effect) for three months, but it is not possible to claim in advance of the tax year for which the person is claiming.

The rules for reporting changes in circumstances are complex, some having to be reported during the year, others dealt with at the end of the year (see Appendix 1). For example, when family circumstances change, like the birth of a child, the tax credit award is adjusted from the date of the change. The new system can have advantages, such as getting childcare costs met when the need arises rather than waiting for the end of a fixed-term award. However, parents have to keep track of changes in hours, earnings and childcare and remember to report significant changes.

A rise in income and the £2,500 'buffer' zone

Income *increases* of less than £2,500 can be ignored when finalising the tax credit award. People claiming later in the year could benefit most from this 'buffer'. It will also benefit people whose income rises during the year more than those whose income is more accurately forecast at the beginning.

For example, a family with £10,000 income last year that rises to £15,000 will have their award adjusted to an income of only £12,500, whilst a family that starts and finishes the year with an annual average income of £15,000 will not experience the £2,500 disregard.[7] For many families the disregard will be worth £925 a year and so it is somewhat inequitable to those who start the year on a higher income and do not see this rise. With some changes (for example, when a couple separate) a fresh claim has to be made and with a new claim the £2,500 disregard does not apply.

The Government estimated that around 60 per cent of the tax credits recipients would have a rise in income between one year and the next, and around 40 per cent would have a rise of £2,000 or less, so many would see no change in their award (although it would be altered the following year).[8] One million people were expected to have a *fall* in income leading to a changed award (they could also ask for an increased award during the year).

Around 750,000 individuals and couples each year were expected to see a *fall in their tax credit award* following a rise in income above the £2,500 threshold (and so at risk of having an overpayment of tax credits if they did not report such a rise when it occurred). Most of these were expected to be either receiving maximum tax credits or at the first income taper (where benefits are withdrawn at 37 pence in the £) – ie, those formerly entitled to WFTC. By April 2004 there were about 1.6 million families in this income range (ie, in work receiving both WTC and CTC), half of whom were lone parents.

In the first year of the new tax credits system, 346,500 in-work families had an increase in their incomes exceeding £2,500 leading to a reduction in their tax credit award.[9] Most of these reported changes were from those families on low/moderate incomes; about two-thirds (213,900) were in the income range £5,060 – £19,999. Only 27,800 were on incomes above £50,000. More may not have reported income increases leading to an overpayment.

Experience in the early months of tax credits suggests that in practice the system was not being responsive to key changes during the year.

Case study

Fall in income

A couple claimed tax credits in February 2003 and received a confirmation letter the same month. Their income is less than it was for the year 2001/02 so they have been trying to contact the Inland Revenue since February. In May 2003 they received a letter from the Inland Revenue asking for more information – all of which was provided with the original claim. They have been unable to get through on the Inland Revenue helpline. They still have not received any payments and as a result have fallen behind with repayments on a loan.

Case study

Change in family composition

A couple, one working and the other on maternity leave, were previously in receipt of WFTC. They claimed tax credits in January 2003. Their second child was born in March. They phoned the Inland Revenue helpline to inform the Inland Revenue about this change of circumstances and also to provide further details of their income that had been requested, but were unable to get through. As a result, they have fallen behind with their rent, council tax and water payments and are having to borrow money from a relative. Their adviser sent a letter of complaint in May and tax credits of £430 per month are now in payment.

Failing to respond to such changes can mean that families are not receiving payments when they need them, which is counterproductive for reducing child poverty.

Responsiveness vs simplicity

The move to an annual system was intended to eliminate unfairness and manipulation of assessments based on a 'snapshot' at a particular point in time, while avoiding the stigma and intrusiveness of weekly means-testing.[10] It was also intended to 'reduce hassle' for claimants. In theory, less frequent assessment of income should reduce the degree to which every time someone gains something it is taken away by the state.[11] However, for low-income families, the longer period may entail greater scope for changes to occur which may affect entitlement (see below).

There is a balance to be struck between responsiveness to need and simplicity and certainty of a longer award period. In theory, tax credits have been designed to give a set award throughout the year but also to be responsive to changes in income or circumstances during the year. The £2,500 buffer is an attempt to introduce some degree of responsiveness into an annual assessment and to minimise the chances of overpayment.[12]

The UK system was designed to avoid some of the problems encountered by similar systems of support for children, especially in Australia and Canada.[13]

In Canada, people have to wait until the next annual assessment before they can receive any additional help after a fall in income (though they can apply to provincial social assistance schemes offering a means-tested safety net as a last resort, used by about 6 per cent of child tax benefit claimants). In contrast, the Australian system requires people to report both the previous year's income and to forecast the current year's. The previous year's income is then used to reconcile their family tax benefit for the previous year and the forecast for the current year is used to estimate awards for the coming tax year.

About a third of Australian families reported an income change during the year. The UK's system of asking for the previous year's income was intended to avoid the Australian problem of asking people to forecast their income for the current year in order for their award to be determined.[14] In the UK and Australia, annual reconciliation can compromise responsiveness as, unless changes are reported and adjusted immediately, payments will not match current income. The Canadian child tax benefit offers greater simplicity, but at the expense of responsiveness. It does not make adjustments during the year for changes in income, but changes in family composition can lead to changes in awards. A fully responsive system might entail weekly adjustments, though for many (better-off) families such a degree of responsiveness may not be necessary.

Responsiveness under the current tax credits system also places an administrative burden on families, in terms of understanding the rules, monitoring their incomes, childcare costs and hours of work, and informing the Inland Revenue. Previous experience of means-tested benefits found that families did not necessarily respond to changes in incomes and circumstances and could delay claiming their entitlement.[15] An annual system may be more familiar to better-off families who are more used to the tax system and who may encounter fewer changes during a year (perhaps having more stable incomes).

Policy options

The CTC and WTC means test is simpler in some ways (for example, the income rules are closer to those used in the tax system) but more complex in others (such as the way some changes have to be reported immediately and some do not).[16] And whilst awards are set to run for 12 months, this does not remain fixed if certain circumstances change. So families will find it hard to know what their entitlement is and why it changes. This is especially likely to affect low-income families, potentially eligible for CTC and WTC with the childcare element and housing benefit, rather than the better-off families entitled to just the family element.

In practice, income testing can never be both simple and responsive; the issue is what should be the balance/trade-off between them.[17] Experience to date suggests that the UK's system generates confusion about what circumstances have to be reported and when. Families may have the uncertainty of not knowing their true entitlement until the end of the year, and many are required to keep records for longer periods than they may have been used to. Responsiveness is important to ensure that child poverty is minimised, as families on low incomes can be more vulnerable to changes (such as job loss) and have fewer savings to tide them over. People may need to claim their entitlement quickly if their circumstances change and income support has been the 'safety net' to ensure that the poorest families have some income. Some of this safety net role (for payments relating to children) will have passed to CTC. The experiences of families brought to CPAG's attention during this first year suggest that the new scheme will need to be more effective to ensure that families receive what they need when they need it.

The Government has said that the operation of the new system will be closely monitored and that it will look to learn lessons for future development.[18]

Future policy options

- Making it clearer to recipients what changes they need to report and the consequences of not doing so. Award notices are often unclear and cover WTC and CTC together.[19] A clear statement could appear on an award notice saying that it should be kept until the final award notice for the year is received, as it will be needed to assist the process of renewing a claim.
- Considering if different rules for changes of circumstances would be appropriate for WTC and CTC if it seems that one is more affected by changes of circumstances than the other. For example, better-off families receiving the family element only might be more used to annual reporting but others, such as those receiving WTC and CTC, might encounter more frequent changes of circumstances.
- Examining whether a move to current year income assessments, basing awards on expected income (similar to the Australian system), would be more responsive to the needs of lower income families with children.
- Expanding the choice of payment options, such as:
  - making weekly payments of CTC where people are also on IS;
  - having a mix of regular and lump-sum payments;
  - allowing better-off families (ie, those in receipt of the family element only) to claim in advance of the tax year and receive a full year's payment, not just three months' backdating.

We now turn to what happens when a change in circumstances has led to an overpayment of tax credits.

Notes

1 Inland Revenue, *Child and Working Tax Credits Quarterly Statistics*, April 2004
2 N Wikeley, 'The New Tax Credits and Appeals', *Benefits* Vol 12 issue 1, 2004
3 *Welfare Benefits and Tax Credits Handbook 2004/05*, Child Poverty Action Group, pp1378-9
4 P Whiteford and others, *Timing it Right? Tax credits and how to respond to income changes*, Joseph Rowntree Foundation, 2003

5 HM Treasury, *The Child and Working Tax Credits: The Modernisation of Britain's Tax and Benefit System*, No 10, 2002
6 Inland Revenue, *New Tax Credits: supporting families, making work pay and tackling poverty*, A consultative document July 2001
7 P Whiteford, J Millar and M Mendelson, *Timing it Right? Tax credits and how to respond to income changes*, Joseph Rowntree Foundation, 2003
8 See note 5
9 See note 1
10 See note 6
11 D Hirsch and D Darton, *Tackling Poverty and Disadvantage*, Joseph Rowntree Foundation, 2003
12 See note 5
13 See for example, note 4
14 See note 5
15 J Millar, 'From Wage Replacement to Wage Supplement: benefits and tax credits', in J Millar (ed) *Understanding Social Security: issues for policy and practice*, The Policy Press, 2003
16 See note 15
17 See note 4
18 See note 5
19 House of Commons *Hansard*, 3 July 2003, col 377 w

Four

Being paid too much: overpayments

Overpayments are an important and inevitable feature of the move to an annual assessment of incomes, described in Chapter 3. This chapter outlines some of the main aspects of overpayments and the consequences of them being recovered, especially during the year (details of the rules can be found in Appendix 2). It also examines the introduction of penalties and the use of additional (or 'top-up') payments made on hardship grounds. Policy options are discussed at the end of the chapter.

Being paid too much

Some 750,000 families a year (about one in eight tax credit recipients) are likely to experience an increase in their incomes leading to a decreased entitlement, many of whom are on low or moderate incomes. Overpayments are 'one of the biggest potential problems' with tax credits administration but there is apparently no figure on the number of people who have reported changes during the year, nor the number of overpayments.[1] The precise scale of the problem may not come to light until after 'end-of-year reconciliations' are made. In particular, there could be a significant risk of overpayments when the first end-of-year reconciliations occur in summer 2004, as decisions in the first year of the new tax credits were based on the claimant's income in 2001/02.

After the introduction of end-of-year reconciliations in Australia there were 12 times more families overpaid compared with previous years, as what counted as an overpayment had changed and families were more likely to underestimate their incomes than overestimate or get them right.[2] The families most affected by overpayments in Australia (and who might similarly be affected in the UK) included:

- families with moderate to average earnings, where entitlement is beginning to be tapered off as income rises, mainly where earnings fluctuate or the second earner increases her/his hours of work;
- families with a partner who starts work and whose income moves above one of the thresholds;
- families with an older child who enters work part-way through the year.

Although the focus of this book is not on the early days of implementation, the administration of tax credits during that time has had an impact on errors and overpayments. During 2003, CPAG encountered official errors resulting from misreading of forms by the Inland Revenue equipment; delays and mistakes in inputting changes of circumstances data into computers; and incorrect backdating. Claimants also reported incorrect information being given to them by advisers, including the Inland Revenue. Such errors could result in recoverable overpayments.

Award notices do not explain how entitlement has been calculated so claimants do not know whether they have been overpaid in error or not.[3] There is no notification about an overpayment as such during the year; the claimant simply receives an adjusted award notice and so may not clearly understand that an overpayment has occurred.

The House of Commons Public Accounts Committee, following concerns about the Inland Revenue's accounts and administration of the tax credits, noted that some recipients of tax credits realised that they were being overpaid and tried to repay the money, but their offers were declined and they were told to repay next year.[4] The Committee reports that this has now been rectified and people can repay if they wish.

There are different rules concerning overpayments at the end of the year and those arising during the course of a year, explained more fully in Appendix 2.

Recovering overpayments

Rules about tax credit overpayments tend to follow tax, rather than social security, principles. The general rule in social security is that payments cannot be recovered unless the overpayment was caused by the claimant's failure to disclose, or misrepresentation of, a material fact. But the Inland Revenue can recover any tax credit overpayment, irrespective of reasons, even if it has occurred because of an official error.[5] The Inland

Revenue position is that overpayments should not be recovered if they were caused by an Inland Revenue mistake and it was reasonable for the claimant to think the award was right. There is a right of appeal against tax credit entitlement decisions, but not against the decision to recover an overpayment, or how much is to be recovered and in what way.[6]

The Inland Revenue has set out the circumstances in which an overpayment will not be recovered in a Code of Practice, though this was not published until late 2003, seven months after the introduction of tax credits.[7]

Case study

Recovery of overpayment after an Inland Revenue error

The claimant was receiving working tax credit (WTC), but then stopped work and claimed income support (IS). She notified the Inland Revenue that she had stopped work, but WTC still continued to be paid. In total she has telephoned the Inland Revenue 51 times to query the ongoing payments. The Inland Revenue has said that all of the overpayment will be recovered, even though it admits that it was an Inland Revenue error that resulted in WTC continuing to be paid.

Overpayments can be recovered from one or both partners if the claim was made jointly. Particular difficulties may arise where a couple separate, as they are both liable for any overpayment.

For claimants who have overpayments discovered 'in-year' there is no maximum limit to the amount by which their weekly amounts can be reduced, which means they can be reduced to nil.[8] There have been reports of increasing problems with the recovery of overpayments during 2003, with the Inland Revenue routinely recovering payments at a rate designed to clear the debt by the end of the tax year.[9] The computer system automatically adjusts awards to recover the likely overpayment from the balance due to claimants by the end of the year.[10] So a large overpayment discovered late in the year might lead to a substantial change in current entitlement.

This recovery of overpayments during the year could have a serioius impact on a family's income, increasing the risk of children falling into poverty. Where payments are reduced to recover an overpayment by the end of the year, a family can be left with an income below what their current entitlement would otherwise be. Especially where an overpayment is discovered shortly before the end of the year, entitlement can be reduced to nil. In effect, this can mean that child tax credit (CTC) payments cease.

For some families, this will create hardship (especially if they are used to weekly budgeting) and may undermine the purpose of CTC being seen as a payment for children if an overpayment has occurred for reasons unrelated to the child.

Additional payments for hardship

If the Inland Revenue agrees that an overpayment was made because of official error, or that reducing/stopping the award will lead to hardship, it has the discretion to make additional (or 'top-up') payments. The Inland Revenue has listed factors that it would expect to take into account in determining how, and what time to give someone, to repay. These include living expenses, bills, savings, previous payment history, and whether there is a child under five or a sick or disabled person in the household whose health could be affected. But in practice hardship is not always accepted.

Case study

Hardship not accepted

A lone parent with two children, one disabled, was awarded CTC and WTC when working 16 hours a week, but was overpaid as a result of the Inland Revenue incorrectly including a disability element in her WTC. She told the Inland Revenue of this straight away. She is no longer working and the overpayment is being recovered from her CTC. She is getting £53 a week instead of £123.55 a week, despite a request to the Inland Revenue to reduce the rate of recovery to prevent hardship.

Additional payments can be made at 90 per cent or 70 per cent of the full entitlement. If someone is only receiving the family element, no such payments are made. Additional payments are likely to be regarded as overpayments at the end of the year.[12] The onus is on individuals to say they are in hardship, so much depends on the quality of information available to the individual claimant.

Rates of recovery

Recovery of an overpayment from a previous tax year can be made by reducing the tax credit award in the current year, adjusting the PAYE code, or by a direct payment. For those whose overpayment is recovered by reducing a current award, the maximum amounts deducted are:

- 10 per cent for claimants receiving the maximum award;
- 25 per cent for claimants receiving less than the maximum, but more than just the family element of CTC;
- 100 per cent for claimants receiving only the family element of CTC.[11]

A percentage deduction rate will disadvantage those receiving the largest awards (because of disability, childcare costs, or being a large family), often the poorest claimants. The jump in deductions from 10 per cent to 25 per cent could produce some dramatic differences in recovery rates for claimants with only marginally higher incomes than those getting the maximum award. This could discourage claimants from taking up employment (see below).

Example

Comparing recovery rates

We compared two families, each headed by a lone parent working 16 hours a week with two children. One family has an annual income of just £10 below the threshold of £5,060 and the other has an income of £140 above the threshold. We assumed that that they both had an overpayment of £2,000 to repay. They receive the same maximum tax credit award of £6,460. Their yearly difference in income is £150 – reduced to £98.20 because of the 37 per cent taper.

The family whose income is below the threshold gets the maximum tax credit award and so would have that reduced by 10 per cent – a weekly deduction of £12.42 (£646 a year). The other family would have the 25 per cent rate applied, resulting in a weekly deduction of £30.81 (£1,602.05 a year). This is a difference of £18.39 a week, when their actual difference in income is only £1.88 a week.

An overpayment of one tax credit can be recovered from the other, making entitlement confusing and uncertain; an overpayment of WTC can wipe out CTC entitlement.

Case study

Overpayment of working tax credit recovered from child tax credit

The claimant is a lone parent with two children and in receipt of disability

> benefits following a stroke. She is self-employed, working over 16 hours a week and receiving both WTC and CTC. She had to reduce her hours as a result of her disability, but delayed informing the Inland Revenue of this – her disability causes her difficulties in managing her affairs. Following her notification, the Inland Revenue delayed revising her tax credits award. An overpayment of WTC occurred and her CTC was stopped for the rest of the year in order to recover it. She is currently disputing the date when she informed the Inland Revenue of her change in hours. Her adviser says that the Inland Revenue is recovering the overpayment without informing her how it arose and without using its discretion not to recover on hardship grounds. The claimant is receiving top-up payments at 90 per cent of her full entitlement.

Tax credits overpayments can, therefore, potentially reduce payments to a greater extent than overpayment of benefits like IS (recovery of IS overpayments are subject to a maximum of £10.80 a week in cases of fraud, £8.10 for other instances).

Penalties

Financial penalties and interest can be added to any overpayment when the overpayment arose if someone has fraudulently or negligently made an incorrect statement or declaration, or supplied incorrect information or evidence (see Appendix 2). In such circumstances, the Inland Revenue can also add interest to all or some of the overpayment, increasing the amount the recipient has to pay. To date there is little evidence on the use of penalties.

Policy options

Overpayments are a new aspect of a new system, so individuals and advisers may need time to understand the new rules and their implications. A key feature is the influence of tax rules on tax credits, affecting families and advisers who may previously have been used to different social security regulations. Another new aspect of tax credits is that the Inland Revenue can negotiate with claimants to settle any appeal against a penalty decision before the hearing, which is a more familiar concept within tax, rather than social security, law and requiring new skills for advisers and individuals. In addition to the impact on families, the House of Commons Public Accounts Committee also noted that, as overpayments are counted as 'tax collected' within the Inland Revenue's accounts, they are not subject to the same accountability to Parliament as are social security benefits (which need Parliamentary approval).[13]

Contrary to the original intention that tax credits should be a more transparent system, the way overpayments are assessed, notified and recovered is opaque. At the very least, the administration of overpayments could be improved to ensure that claimants and advisers have a better understanding of how entitlement is, and will be, affected. For example, the Public Accounts Committee recommended that the Inland Revenue should explain to those affected how recovery and non-recovery of tax credit overpayments took account of the implications for other benefits, such as housing benefit.[14]

In the longer term, policy changes are needed to ensure that the rules on overpayments support the Government's objectives of reducing child poverty. In particular, the House of Commons Work and Pensions Select Committee recommended that: overpayments arising from official error should not be recovered inappropriately; overpayments should not be recovered where this would cause hardship or damage work incentives; the Inland Revenue should evaluate whether additional 'top-up' payments are adequate to avoid hardship when awards are adjusted during the year; and the right of appeal against decisions to recover overpayments should be reinstated.[15]

Future policy options

- Making immediate changes to improve the administration of overpayments. This includes clearer award notices so that people know to what and the amount to which they are entitled, and what circumstances might alter their award. Overpayments should be notified separately, giving information about how they have arisen, the likely means of recovery and the additional top-up payments that can be made if hardship occurs.
- Ending in-year recovery of overpayments, as full recovery of an overpayment within the year can undermine child policy objectives. The Inland Revenue should consider taking recovery action only at the end of the year when full reconciliation is undertaken.

- Reducing the recovery rate of overpayments so that overpayments are collected more slowly, but leaving families with CTC payments that are only slightly below their entitlement. An alternative would be to pay top-up payments automatically.
- Ending the right to recover overpayments that have clearly resulted from official error and introducing statutory tests for recoverability.
- Reinstating the right to appeal a decision on tax credit overpayments and on whether they should be recovered.

Next, we consider the circumstances when people may be paid too little.

Notes

1 House of Commons Work and Pensions Committee, *Child Poverty in the UK*, Second Report of Session 2003/04, HC 85-1, 2004

2 P Whiteford and others, *Timing it Right? Tax credits and how to respond to income changes*, Joseph Rowntree Foundation, 2003

3 S Clarke, 'Tax Credit Overpayments: rights and wrongs', *Welfare Rights Bulletin 177* December 2003

4 House of Commons Committee of Public Accounts, *Inland Revenue: tax credits*, Fourteenth Report of Session 2003/04, HC 89, 2004

5 N Wikeley, 'The New Tax Credits and Appeals', *Benefits* Vol 12 issue 1, 2004

6 S Osborne, 'Tax Credit Overpayments: official guidance', *Welfare Rights Bulletin 177* December 2003

7 Inland Revenue, *What Happens if We Have Paid You Too Much Tax Credit?* Code of Practice COP26, 2003

8 See note 3

9 G Vaux, 'It's Pay Back Time', *Community Care* 5-11, February 2004

10 Citizens Advice, *Evidence*, January 2004

11 *Welfare Benefits and Tax Credits Handbook 2004/05*, Child Poverty Action Group p1392

12 See note 11, p1390

13 See note 4

14 See note 4

15 See note 1, para 121

Five

Being paid too little: underpayments

This chapter looks at the available evidence about mistakes that can lead to people being underpaid tax credits and the quality of service experienced by claimants in the first year. Also, crucially for child poverty, the importance of people taking up their entitlement is examined, followed by some suggested policy reforms.

Inland Revenue errors

Before the tax credits system was introduced in 2003 claims were decided within the target clearance time (90 per cent in five days) but accuracy targets were missed.[1] The National Audit Office 'qualified' the Inland Revenue's accounts for the year 2002/03 because of the high levels of overpayment.[2] In addition, the Inland Revenue made errors in processing claims and the accuracy rate in 2003 was lower than in previous years (85.2 per cent compared with a target accuracy of 93 per cent). Potential overpayment amounted to £90.8 million and potential underpayment £87.6 million. The Public Accounts Committee has stated that this level of error is unacceptable.[3]

Error rates for working families' tax credit were estimated to be 23 per cent, though this was expected to be halved with the new tax credits because of the extensive cross-checking by computer technology.[4] However, the Inland Revenue will only be able to get an error rate for the new tax credits population when it carries out a full random programme on a complete set of finalised awards for 2004/05.[5]

Even with halving the error rate, this suggests that mistakes could be made in around one in ten decisions. With six million recipients and an estimated cost of £16 billion in 2003/04, this might translate into almost 660,000 families facing inaccurate awards to the value of £1.76 billion.[6]

For many families it will not be clear that a mistake has been made until their award is finalised at the end of the year, though adjustments can only be backdated for three months.

Below are examples of mistakes made in calculating entitlement that have led to claimants being underpaid.

Case study

Errors

A couple with one earner made an initial claim for tax credits that included their one child. The Inland Revenue was notified of the birth of their second child and their reduced income. The claimant was not able to get through on the Inland Revenue helpline and so went in person to the local Inland Revenue office, which at first seemed reluctant to help. After the claimant broke down in tears, the details were taken and an emergency payment covering six weeks was made – this process took three hours. An award notice eventually arrived, but payment was still due. A second award notice arrived showing an incorrect change of income and so a 'nil' entitlement. The claimant contacted the helpline and made a complaint. The Inland Revenue said a new award would be made in three to four weeks and advised the couple to claim an emergency payment from the local office.

Case study

Errors

A claimant was told by the Inland Revenue that she was not entitled to any tax credits, but an adviser subsequently calculated that she had an entitlement of over £200 a week.

Where families have been underpaid the Inland Revenue can make a single payment to cover any outstanding amounts owed.

The expectation is that when income falls (leading to an underpayment) people will automatically report this to the Inland Revenue, but evidence from take-up of benefits suggests that people do not always claim what they are entitled to, and so some people may not report changes until the end of the year.[7] This can result in some people losing money, since tax credits can only be backdated for three months. As these tax credits are intended as the main support for families with children in poor families this could have considerable consequences for their income and living standards.

Complaints and compensation

People who are dissatisfied with the way their claim has been handled can complain. Another Inland Revenue Code of Practice sets out a complaints procedure, stating that when mistakes have been made they will be corrected and any costs incurred as a result (such as extra postage or phone calls) can be reimbursed.[8] Additional payments for worry and distress can be made, ranging from £25 to £500. If a complaint is handled badly or takes an unreasonable amount of time to deal with, compensation payments of between £25 and £500 can also be made. Between April and September 2003 approximately 1,600 compensation awards were paid, with an average value of £30.[9]

However, there was no official campaign to draw attention to compensation arrangements; the Public Accounts Committee recommended that the effectiveness of the compensation scheme should be monitored and if numbers were low, a campaign should be targeted at those most likely to have been disadvantaged.

Case study

Poor quality of service

A lone parent stopped work in October 2003 and informed the Inland Revenue helpline. She was told that her award could not be changed until her employer got in touch with the Inland Revenue, but she was not told about the possibility of an overpayment occurring. The claimant's later tax credit awards indicated that she was still working, so she informed the Inland Revenue again that she was not. She continued to receive child tax credit (CTC) of £38.08 and income support until an award notice in November showed an overpayment of working tax credit (WTC) of £378.86. Her CTC was reduced to £14.72 per week. The claimant contacted the helpline and was told to go to her local tax office for a hardship payment. She incurred travel costs getting to the office, which was not aware of the existence of hardship payments. The claimant contacted a citizens advice bureau. The adviser was told by the tax credits office that the local office could not access that part of the system but that a memo would be sent to the supervisor to 'move things along' and that the adviser would be called back later. The adviser was not called back and was unable to ascertain who, or which section of the tax credits office, was responsible for additional payments.

The importance of take-up

One of the main disadvantages of income-related benefits and tax credits is that people have to apply for them. Not all do so, either because they do not know they are eligible or because they choose not to do so. In contrast, benefits like child benefit are claimed by virtually all of those entitled. Hence, the success or failure of CTC in reducing child income poverty will depend to a large degree on what proportion of entitled families claim.

The Government's original estimate of CTC take-up was 90 per cent, as nine out of ten families with children would be eligible and 5.75 million families would receive it (out of 7.25 million families with children in the UK).[10] In effect, 10 per cent of families would have an annual household income that would be too high to receive CTC.[11] However, by September 2003 the numbers claiming reached 5.8 million (announced as 95 per cent of all those expected to be reached over the whole year); by January 2004, this had risen to six million and was seen as the figure expected for the year.[12] The end-of-year figure does indeed show six million recipients.

However, this does not seem to be a 'take-up' estimate *per se*. The 90 per cent estimate was based on the official Family Resources Survey and reliable information from which to make more precise estimates of take-up is not expected to be available until the data for 2003/04 has been produced and analysed, which is not expected until late in 2004.[13]

Under the previous system, in 2001/02 between 71 per cent and 74 per cent of those eligible claimed the former working families' tax credit. These proportions were higher for people who would have been entitled to the previous family credit had it simply been increased with inflation (81–87 per cent), and for lone parents (82–88 per cent) compared with couples (59–64 per cent).[14] This might suggest that those most likely to claim are in the lower income groups (with the most to gain from claiming) rather than those entitled only to the family element of CTC. The former children's tax credit (roughly equivalent to the family element) was received by an estimated 72 per cent of those eligible.

However, trends cannot simply be extrapolated from previous systems as the post-2003 system is calculated in a different way, so it will be harder to measure take-up accurately in future, as it will be hard to pin down entitlements. For example, people may enter and leave eligibility as their circumstances change during a year, so it is questionable whether or not they should be counted as receiving tax credits if they only receive one payment during the course of a year.

Eligibility will also depend on families' understanding of what they are likely to receive under particular circumstances, and the confusion about what changes affect entitlement could depress take-up rates. The image of the Inland Revenue and tax credits based on people's early experiences could also have an impact on their take-up.[15]

A positive aspect of tax credits that might encourage their take-up is that payments of CTC go to most families, so there should be less 'stigma' attached to claiming. Another is that payments are made to the main carer. But the problems of administration and how overpayments are tackled could have a negative effect.

Policy options

The administration of the new tax credits was intended to be simpler and more transparent. For example, there is a single application form for both CTC and WTC rather than two. Yet the complexity of the new system means it is likely to take time for advisers and claimants to become used to it and, in particular, individuals may not understand their entitlement or the basis of their actual award. This will be essential to ensure that the poorest families receive their entitlement.

The quality of service is also important and the experience of the first year may reflect some of the implementation problems resulting from computer failure. The National Audit Office noted that the new tax credits system affected the stability, speed and availability of claims processing, which may not be fully resolved until late 2004. It also concluded that as well as catching up on backlogs and day-to-day maintenance, there are major issues for the Inland Revenue to control for 2003/04, including ensuring that the problems with the start of the new scheme have not led to errors in detailed information about claims or payments. Hence, a poor start could have a knock-on effect on processing claims well into 2004/05.

Future policy options

- Considering what may be needed to improve the quality of decision making and the number of errors.
- Extending backdating to 12 months where an award should have been made, or made at a higher rate, where this was a result of an official error.

- Revising award notices to make them clearer. This could include simple back-up leaflets explaining issues such as the right to appeal and to complain; how to read the award notice; what to do if the award looks wrong; rules about reporting changes; and how overpayments and underpayments can be dealt with.
- Emphasising the child poverty targets and the role of CTC in reducing child poverty in staff training and guidance.
- Developing a face-to-face service as well as a telephone service to increase take-up and improve the quality of the service.
- Publicising take-up estimates on a regular basis and undertaking partnerships with voluntary sector agencies to ensure that claims are made and processed quickly.
- Considering whether the level of compensation payments could mirror penalty amounts as an incentive to improve the quality of the service.
- Reviewing current IT arrangements with a view to improving the quality and speed of service for applicants.

Notes

1 Inland Revenue, *Annual Report*, December 2003

2 National Audit Office, *Standard Report on the Accounts of the Inland Revenue 2002/03*, 2003

3 House of Commons Committee of Public Accounts, *Inland Revenue: tax credits*, Fourteenth Report of Session 2003/04, HC 89, 2004

4 Sir Nicholas Montague, minutes of evidence, Public Accounts Committee 3 December 2003

5 House of Commons *Hansard*, 5 February 2004, col 1003w

6 Based on 11 per cent of both figures.

7 P Whiteford and others, *Timing it Right? Tax credits and how to respond to income changes*, Joseph Rowntree Foundation, 2003

8 Inland Revenue, *Putting Things Right: how to complain*, Code of practice COP1, 2003

9 House of Commons *Hansard*, 19 November 2003, col1100w

10 M Brewer, *The New Tax Credits*, Briefing Note 35, Institute for Fiscal Studies, 2003

11 House of Commons *Hansard*, 14 April 2003, col 536w

12 Inland Revenue Press Notice, 10 September 2003 and 30 January 2004

13 House of Commons *Hansard*, 6 November 2003, col 804w

14 Inland Revenue, *Working Families' Tax Credit Estimate of Take-up Rates in 2001–2002*, 2003

15 See note 2

Six

Relationship with other benefits

This chapter considers some of the interactions between tax credits and other benefits. In particular, the rules on tax credits as 'qualifying benefits' to other benefits and services like free prescriptions and free school meals are examined. This is followed by a discussion on the relationship between tax credits and benefits like income support (IS) and housing benefit (HB), and concludes with some suggestions for further policy change.

'Passported' benefits and rules

Before 2003, receipt of a means-tested benefit or tax credit could also be a 'passport' to other benefits or services, such as free school meals and free prescriptions. There are arguments for and against tying entitlements together. The advantage for administrators and for individuals is that there is no need for a separate test of entitlement. However the disadvantages include complexity and the withdrawal of in-kind benefits, which (like free health care and food stamps in the US) can create a poverty trap.[1] People just above the income level for a benefit like IS that also carries eligibility for passported benefits like free prescriptions can also lose out disproportionately; not only have they just missed out on IS but they also lost the value of the passported benefits. This also underlines the importance of take-up, as non-receipt of one benefit like child tax credit (CTC) can mean that access to other passported benefits is lost.

With the change to the new tax credits, a person losing IS or jobseeker's allowance (JSA) because her/his entitlement has been incorporated into CTC could, in effect, be worse off if s/he also lost passported benefits. People on IS can be eligible for:

- free milk and vitamins;
- free school meals;

- help with the cost of prison visits;
- health benefits (including prescriptions and fares to hospital);
- social fund community care grants and budgeting loans.

People on CTC can be eligible for:

- a Sure Start maternity grant if CTC is payable at a rate greater than the family element;
- a social fund funeral payment if CTC is payable at a rate greater than the family element;
- health benefits (including prescriptions and fares to hospital) if annual income is below £14,600;
- education benefits such as free school meals if annual income is below £13,480.

In effect, this means that people no longer receiving IS, even if their incomes are low enough for them to be on the maximum CTC, will not be able to apply for discretionary grants and loans from the social fund.

Problems proving entitlement to passported benefits

Payment of tax credits via a bank account and the lack of clear award notices can mean some claimants have difficulty proving their entitlement to passported benefits.

Case study

Sure Start maternity grant refused

The claimant is a new parent entitled to CTC at more than the family element, but she has not received an award notice. A Sure Start maternity grant was refused because she had no proof of entitlement to a qualifying benefit. She was advised to claim as soon as gets the award notice, but she needs to buy baby things now.

In the case of exemption from NHS prescription charges, the Inland Revenue sends data to the prescription pricing authority to issue certificates of exemption. However, there does not seem to be a similar arrangement between the Inland Revenue and local education authorities in relation to free school meals, which means that entitlement depends on having a correct tax credits award notice.

Case study

Free school meals refused

The claimant is a lone parent with two children. She stopped working in August and informed the Inland Revenue. Her working tax credit (WTC) stopped and CTC continued. The Inland Revenue sent her a revised award notice stating that she was entitled to WTC of £1,100 for the tax year. The claimant queried this with Inland Revenue helpline and was advised that WTC must remain in the revised award notice as it is the WTC that has been paid to her in this tax year. She has been told by her local education authority that her children are not eligible for free school meals because of the WTC award. She explained that she was not working anymore, but the local education authority will only make a decision based on the award notice.

Passported benefits can have a role to play in reducing child poverty, as they can reduce the costs that a family has to incur. The cash value of income in kind, like free school meals, is counted as income in the *Households Below Average Income* statistics. The impact of an overpayment reducing an award to nil on passported benefits is unclear.[2] However, it is likely that someone might also lose passported benefits.

Evidence suggests that existing claimants may know of passported benefits; three-quarters of working families' tax credit (WFTC) recipients used one of the benefits to which they were passported from WFTC (such as free prescriptions) and more were aware of them.[3] Free prescriptions and dental care were the most frequently used. However, knowledge cannot always be assumed; CPAG has learned that some advisers have discovered that their clients have not always received the Inland Revenue leaflet on passported benefits with their award notices.

Relationship with income support and jobseeker's allowance

As noted in Chapter 1, receipt of IS entitles someone to the maximum CTC. The relationship with IS and JSA differed in the first year of tax credit operations from subsequent years.

- During 2003/04, both CTC and WTC were counted in full as income for IS/JSA. This was a problem where someone had deductions from her/his CTC for a tax credits overpayment, as the amount of CTC taken

into account as income for IS was the full CTC entitlement, not the actual amount s/he was being paid. As a result some claimants with children had their incomes reduced below IS levels during that year.
- From April 2004 CTC does not count as income for IS/JSA.

In 2004/05, the final phase of separating children and adult payments will take place. The child and adult elements of IS and JSA will be separated out so that the child elements must be claimed through CTC and the adult allowance through IS/JSA. Current IS recipients will have child elements transferred to CTC. This will leave just the amounts for adults and housing costs within an individual's entitlement. Families with children will, therefore, have to claim two benefits – IS/JSA for themselves and CTC for their children. The effect of this change is unlikely to be clear until well into the second year of operation. Any assessment of the impact of tax credits on child income poverty for people receiving IS, the impact of having two separate assessments for child and adult payments, and the transparency of CTC specifically as a payment for children, requires further analysis.

Relationship with housing benefit

HB is a means-tested benefit to help people on low incomes (whether or not in work) pay for rent. The higher the income, the lower the HB.

People on IS and JSA can usually receive the maximum HB. Those with other incomes have HB entitlement calculated on a weekly, family means test, similar to the way IS is calculated. People receiving tax credits who need to claim HB, therefore, have to undergo two different means tests:

- tax credits, based on the previous year's income and on gross earnings (subject to a disregard of rises of up to £2,500 between years), with a withdrawal rate of 37 per cent; *and*
- HB, based on the last five weeks or two months' gross earnings less deductions, with some disregards on earnings and for people receiving WTC.

Unlike IS, HB and council tax benefit (CTB) will continue to include amounts for children in claims post-2004. Tax credits are taken into account as income for HB/CTB.

CTC and WTC count in full as income for HB and, as noted in Chapter 1, the rate at which HB is withdrawn as income rises can increase marginal deduction rates. Hence a £1 gain from work can be considerably reduced (often by 96 pence in the £ for people receiving both HB and CTB).[4]

Example

Impact of housing benefit withdrawal

A lone parent with one child under 11 and paying rent at £47.52 per week has a weekly income on IS of £171.24 before housing costs (£111.82 after housing costs). She also receives £16.05 child benefit per week.

If she were to get a part-time job with gross earnings of £90 a week, she would receive:

CTC	£38.08
WTC	£57.89
HB	£ 3.39

Her net income before housing costs would be £205.18 (after housing costs £145.76). The marginal deduction rate at this level of income would be 72.3 per cent.

If her earnings increased by £5 to £95 a week she would receive:

CTC	£38.08
WTC	£57.89
HB	£ 0.83

Her net income before housing costs would be £206.56 (after housing costs £147.14). The marginal deduction rate at this level of income would be 103.7 per cent – ie, at this point she would lose more than she gains.

However, on earnings of £100 a week she would receive:

CTC	£38.08
WTC	£56.70

Her net income before housing costs would be £208.49 (after housing costs £149.07). The marginal deduction rate at this level of income would be 58.8 per cent as she is no longer entitled to HB.

Policy options

People on the lowest incomes are more likely to be entitled to more than one benefit or tax credit and therefore face more interaction between them. This means that entitlement is more complex and difficult to understand, or that the rules for one may not be consistent with the other. It can also mean that changes to entitlement to one benefit or tax credit can affect other interrelated or passported benefits, such as where entitlement to CTC is withdrawn. People with the highest entitlements (and so on the lowest incomes) are likely to be more affected by these interrelationships than better-off families who are only entitled to the family element of CTC. Simplifying the system could, therefore, improve take-up and access to help for the families with children who need the most support and help meet child income poverty targets.

Short-term policy options

- Improving the notification of tax credits awards for passported benefits. This includes clearly identifying the different tax credit awards in the notice and referring to those passported benefits which could be claimed.
- Making entitlement to passported benefits automatic. Experience to date suggests that, because some passporting arrangements require people to make a separate claim, delays in entitlement to passported benefits can occur. This can be compounded if people do not have the correct award notice or cannot prove their tax credit entitlement. One option would be to make all passporting arrangements automatic. For example, the Inland Revenue could send notices to relevant authorities like local education authorities. Guidance to the relevant authorities that deal with passported benefits may also help.
- Simplifying the current passporting arrangements for health and education benefits, so that, for example, people could qualify for passported benefits if they are in receipt of CTC, except where only the family element is payable (better-off families). At the same time, to help the poorest families with children who may be on incomes only just above the IS level, allow people in receipt of the maximum CTC to become eligible for discretionary social fund grants and loans for essential items at times of need.

- Tackling further HB anomalies, such as the income calculations and earnings disregards. Earnings disregards can be a particular problem where housing costs are high, leading to suggestions that a higher earnings disregard could apply in those areas (such as London) or some kind of 'London weighting' or disregard within WTC.[5]

In the longer term, the new tax credits also present an opportunity to rethink the relationship with HB.[7] The Government is already experimenting with the introduction of 'shopping incentives' (often suggested as an alternative to rent restrictions) by piloting a flat-rate housing allowance, set locally and taking account of income and family size. However, while some people may be able to take up cheaper accommodation, others may be unable to do so and be worse off as a result, having to find the shortfall from other income.[6] Longer-term options also have the attraction of potentially extending help to low income owner-occupiers.

Long-term policy options

- A 'housing credit', which would integrate into the new tax credit system like the current childcare tax credit element within WTC. This would mean that, as incomes rise, the housing credit tapers first, followed by WTC (excluding childcare) and then the childcare element. This has the advantage of simplicity and reducing marginal tax rates, but the disadvantage of extending tapers further up the income scale.
- A 'partial housing credit', which would complement rather than replace HB. A flat-rate allowance would be added to tax credits and households with higher costs would apply to HB for help with the remainder. This would reduce the numbers of people getting both HB and tax credits.
- Another alternative might be to set the rate of other tax credits at a level that could meet housing costs – though with the variability of housing costs across Britain it would either be too low for some or too high for others.

Notes

1 D Hirsch, *A Credit to Children: the UK's radical reform of children's benefits in an international perspective*, Joseph Rowntree Foundation, 2000

2 S Clarke, 'Tax Credit Overpayments: rights and wrongs', *Welfare Rights Bulletin 177*, December 2003

3 M Barnes and others, *Families and Children in Britain: findings from the 2002 Families and Children Study (FACS)*, Department for Work and Pensions Research Report 206, 2004

4 Department for Work and Pensions, *Tax Benefit Model Tables April 2003*, 2004

5 P Bivand and others, *Making Work Pay in London: a report by the Centre for Economic and Social Inclusion*, 2003

6 Rahilly, 'Housing Benefit and Work Disincentives', *Industrial Law Journal* Vol 33 No 1, March 2004

7 P Kemp and others, *Housing Benefit Reform: next steps*, Joseph Rowntree Foundation, 2002

Seven

Childcare and child poverty

This chapter considers the contribution that childcare can make to reducing child poverty, both in helping parents to work and in improving outcomes for children. Some of the remaining obstacles for low-income families in obtaining childcare, notably the costs and the (still) limited supply of childcare places are also examined. Current arrangements for help with childcare costs are more fully explained in Appendix 3.

The contribution of childcare to reducing poverty

Provision of good quality affordable childcare can help to combat poverty in two ways: by helping the parents to work (and so increase their incomes) and by helping children to develop skills that may reduce the chances of them growing up to be poor.

Employment

The Government's strategy has been to reduce poverty and social exclusion by increasing the opportunities for parents to take paid work, which has included initiatives to increase available and affordable childcare. Childcare is one of the most common barriers to work reported by parents without a job, and finding affordable and appropriate childcare remains one of the most significant barriers for lone parents. Hence, if better childcare provision were available, more mothers would be likely to work; two-thirds have said they would prefer to work or study if they had suitable childcare provision.[1]

Since the launch of the National Childcare Strategy in 1998, places for over 1.3 million children have been created, putting the Government on course to meet its target of 1.6 million places by 2004 and over two million by 2006.[2] The Sure Start programme for children under age four now operates in 500 areas, reaching 400,000 children.[3] Children's centres are being introduced (offering integrated early years, day care, health and parenting support) in the 20 per cent most deprived areas.

Since 1997 the employment rate of lone parents has increased by 7 per cent so that now, for the first time, more than 50 per cent of lone parents are in work.[4] Some of this increase is due to the improved financial incentives from the introduction of working families' tax credit (WFTC) and childcare tax credit.[5] Further expansion of the supply of childcare could potentially increase women's employment rates by almost the same percentage.[6]

Impact on children

Good quality childcare can have a positive impact on child development; one review suggested that high quality childcare can have the strongest effects on child development for children from disadvantaged backgrounds, especially if associated with home visits.[7] Formal (rather than informal) childcare seems to be associated with better cognitive outcomes.[8] Early education can enhance children's intellectual and social development, with disadvantaged children benefiting significantly from good quality pre-school experiences.[9] Pilots of early excellence centres, catering for children from a mix of social backgrounds, also seem to reduce rates of child protection orders and children being 'looked after' by the local authority.[10] In the longer term, early childhood interventions can boost confidence and social skills that might be factors leading to better educational outcomes and earning potential in adulthood.[11]

However, many families currently use informal childcare, like friends and relatives, often someone known and trusted by parents to provide the quality of care comparable to their own. This falls outside of the criteria for help with meeting the costs of approved childcare. Families more likely to use informal care include lone parents (especially during school holidays) and parents from black and minority ethnic communities, suggesting the need for a more diverse childcare workforce and forms of provision to reflect the range of cultural values.[12] Families use childcare less often when mothers do not work.[13] In contrast, parents working for 30 hours or more were more likely to use eligible childcare, as were better-off families.[14] This suggests that if more formal care were available (and it was culturally appropriate and accessible) more families would use it.

The costs of childcare

One of the barriers to using formal care is its cost, particularly for large families or those with younger children. A Department for Work and Pensions study has shown that, compared with school-age children, pre-school childcare was more likely to be formal provision (and so eligible for the childcare tax credit), as well as being more expensive.[15] The average weekly cost of pre-school care was £43 greater for eligible care and £9 greater for informal care compared with the weekly rates for a school-aged child.

The Daycare Trust has found that pre-school and playgroups cost £3 to £5 a session (ie, morning or afternoon), which may have to be paid for half a term in advance.[16] A full-time nursery place for a child aged under two can cost almost £7,000 a year, higher in London and the South East. Typical weekly costs for a full-time place in 2004 in England were:

Nursery (under 2)	£134
Nursery (over 2)	£123
Childminder (under 2)	£121
Childminder (over 2)	£120
After-school club (15 hours)	£35

Compared with England, costs seem to be lower in Scotland, where a third of parents were paying less than £20 a week and a fifth paying more than £70 a week in 1999.[17] Just under a quarter of paying parents said they would have to stop their childcare use if costs rose by 25 per cent (and conversely if costs reduced by 25 per cent they would use more).

Costs have been rising in recent years (5 per cent between this year and last). The Daycare Trust estimates that parents pay three-quarters of the cost of childcare, with the Government paying the rest with a small contribution from employers; in 2002, parents paid £2.2 billion to the day nursery industry.

Help with childcare costs

Families can receive help with the costs of eligible childcare (mainly formal) through the childcare element of working tax credit (WTC) and as a disregard in housing benefit and some other benefits (eligibility is explained in Appendix 3). Help is available for up to 70 per cent of actual childcare costs of up to £135 for one child, or £200 a week for two or more children. These amounts were not uprated in 2004 (so representing a real-terms cut). In April 2004, the average amount allowed for childcare costs was £50 a week.[18]

Table 7.1

Families with working tax credit awards including the childcare element

	Numbers receiving the childcare element (000s)	Average weekly help with childcare costs
United Kingdom	317.7	£49.66
England	263.3	£50.14
North East	13.3	£47.15
North West	48.6	£48.41
Yorkshire and Humberside	30.0	£46.36
East Midlands	24.9	£48.76
West Midlands	32.0	£47.86
East	22.0	£50.85
London	33.0	£63.66
South East	33.0	£50.78
South West	26.5	£44.88
Wales	14.2	£44.65
Scotland	28.5	£46.28
Northern Ireland	8.9	£54.77

Source: *Inland Revenue Tax Credit Statistics*, April 2004

Having help with childcare costs has widened the scope of affordable childcare for many parents, such as using their first choice of provider, moving from informal to formal care, and for longer hours.[19]

Take-up of the childcare element

Since the introduction of the new tax credits, almost 60 per cent more families received help with childcare costs (317,700 families in the first year).[20] However, only 15 per cent of couples and 25 per cent of lone parents receiving WTC also receive the childcare element.

Take-up of the childcare element seems to have been limited by both the eligibility criteria and the supply of childcare. Research has found that where eligible childcare is used, take-up seems fairly high (85 per cent of families receiving the former WFTC and incurring eligible costs were receiving help with childcare).[21] Qualitative research suggested that those not claiming were either not using any childcare, or using ineligible childcare; having to pay the 30 per cent contribution was a discouraging factor but would not deter claims as people tended to feel better off by being in employment.[22] Availability of childcare was a bigger obstacle than affordability. That research did, however, note that the eligibility requirement on both partners (see Appendix 3) was the reason for 60 per cent of disallowances in August 2002.

As part of WTC the childcare element is only payable to working families, excluding those studying or out of work (though families on maternity or adoption leave are now eligible). So when WTC ceases (such as at the end of a job, or where someone's hours reduce), help with the costs of a childcare place stops, so parents either have to give up the place or find other means of funding it while they look for work.

Even with the childcare tax credit, childcare remains expensive with only the better-off likely to afford their first childcare choice – for lower income parents there is likely to be a trade-off between quality and affordability.

The supply of childcare

Although there has been an expansion of childcare places, there is still only one childcare place for every four children under age eight (down from one in nine in 1997).[23] Whilst 626,000 new childcare places have been created in England, 301,000 have closed and around one in seven parents said there was no local choice for their child.[24] Only half of new providers know what they will do when their start-up funding ends – many still fail to cover their costs. This suggests that more needs to be done to create a stable financial environment for childcare providers and to meet parental and government demand. There are, however, enough early education places to give a free part-time place to all four-year-olds whose parents want one.

The Government's approach of targeting deprived areas is likely to reach some target groups, but these areas may have fewer employment opportunities, and in some localities a disadvantaged area can include pockets of affluence, which push up childcare costs.[25] More places are likely to be needed across the board as better-off families may be taking up places in formal childcare (which are eligible for the childcare tax credit) as they can afford it, rather than lower income families who would qualify for help with childcare costs.[26]

A study of parents' demand for childcare found that:

- one in four parents would like to use some type of childcare but were unable to get it;
- three-fifths who wanted to use formal childcare had not done so in the past year, which suggests that if more were available it would be used;
- demand for formal childcare was more likely to be from lone parents, workless households, low-income families and families living in deprived areas (the latter being more than one and a half times less likely to have used formal childcare than those living in better-off areas).[27]

For lone parents, the greater use of informal care may be dictated by what is available, the lack of formal childcare places constraining demand.[28] More lone parents might use formal childcare if there were more places, prompting the move towards 'childcare tasters'. The large proportion of families using no care or only informal care suggests that there may be considerable scope for expansion in the use of childcare.[29]

Policy options

The UK and Ireland are unusual in having a large 'for profit' sector in the provision of childcare; the National Childcare Strategy relies on the private and voluntary sectors to fill the gaps in provision, with help with childcare costs making these places more affordable for low-income parents.[30] In 2001, fewer than 300,000 children were using services paid for by the local authority – this is now only 6 per cent of the childcare market. Market forces can create unbalanced markets, with childcare provision almost entirely determined by ability to pay.[31]

Universal childcare for children aged between one and four has been estimated by PriceWaterhouseCoopers to cost £10 billion, though there are gains from increased tax and national insurance arising from a higher proportion of working mothers.[32] However, that estimate does not take into account any of the social or longer-term financial gains in relation to reducing child poverty. Having a more universal system would also have the advantage of simplifying the role of tax credits and assisting parents into employment.

Other countries tend to adopt one of four approaches.[33]

- Subsidising childcare itself, so charges are below the market rate (for example, most countries in Europe except the UK, childcare in Sweden and France being cheapest).
- Reducing or rebating charges according to income.
- Mitigating extra costs by having higher cash benefits for families with pre-school children (for example, Australia).
- Offsetting some of the costs via the tax system.

Sweden has a national childcare fee (so the costs are the same everywhere).

The increasing cost of childcare has led some organisations to suggest that the proportion of childcare costs covered should be raised from the current 70 per cent, with more help given to childcare costs of larger families, and some relaxation of the rules about who is eligible. The Institute for Fiscal Studies (IFS) has modelled a range of options, including the following.[34]

- Doubling the effective ceilings for childcare costs to £189 for families with one child and to £280 for families with two or more. The impact of this option is small in terms of number and costs (as most families spend less than the ceiling).
- Increasing the proportion of costs covered to 100 per cent. This increases the numbers eligible and also the cost (over £317 million).
- Including informal care as eligible would expand the numbers eligible but would cost less (£263 million) as informal care is less expensive.
- Introducing a cash voucher of either (a) £1.80 or (b) £2.67[35] per child for each hour of care (formal or informal), with a maximum number of eligible care hours equal to the prime carer's working hours. In effect, this could cover more costs than the current 70 per cent and include payments for informal care. Option (b) would cost £382 million and increase the numbers eligible to 210,000.
- Reducing the working hours limit to any hours a week. This is likely to

have limited impact, mainly because families working less than 16 hours are less likely to use childcare.

- Raising the income threshold for means-testing to £189 a week. This would have a moderate impact, increasing numbers to 169,000 and the cost to £270 million.
- Means-testing only the prime carer (removing the couple element). This could triple the numbers claiming and quadruple the cost to £727 million.
- Removing all means-testing. This would increase numbers eligible to 584,000 and have a very large effect on costs (£1,137 million).

The IFS comments that if children benefit from childcare it should be available to poorer families. Without government intervention families may have inadequate information or may not be able to afford childcare. In addition, the childcare market may be limited and so direct measures to increase the supply of providers may be necessary (such as in the Government's National Childcare Strategy). However, there may be an issue about the balance of government support towards (a) helping parents with the costs of childcare (demand) and (b) helping to extend childcare provision (supply). The same amount of money that it costs to remove means-testing (about £1billion) could perhaps double the Sure Start programme which provides help to children under five in disadvantaged areas.[36]

Future policy options

- Extending the geographical coverage of children's centres. As almost half of poor families do not live in the 20 per cent most deprived areas chosen for children's centres, the Work and Pensions Select Committee recommended that these centres should be rolled out to the 30 per cent most deprived areas by 2006.
- Encouraging the development and use of formal (good quality) childcare, or at least increasing the proportion of formal care used. This could include prioritising expanding early years provision for children under three, which is often the most difficult to obtain and the most expensive.[37] It may also, perhaps, be the most important from a child poverty perspective, as by age two damage to educational development may have been done: 60 per cent of children from low-income groups who perform less well on child development tests at that age

did not improve by age 10, and differences at 42 months strongly predict final educational qualifications.[38]

In the longer term, if childcare is to contribute more directly to the reduction in child poverty there are questions about whether government support should be directed towards greater provision of (free or low-cost) formal childcare or helping parents to pay the market costs of existing provision. There is a case for a package of greater supply of formal childcare and early years provision in all areas, available to all parents who want it, and which is either free or at reduced rate for low-income families. One of the key questions is the extent to which parents should make a financial contribution towards childcare. Arguably, 30 per cent is too high, certainly for low-income families.

One possible option might be to de-couple the childcare tax credit from WTC, which would help non-working parents as well as those who are not working enough hours to qualify for WTC. This would allow a review of rules such as the percentage of costs covered, the threshold at which contributions increase and the rate of withdrawal as income rises. This could also be done in conjunction with extending paid parental leave so that when children are very young parents can provide the care themselves if they choose.

Notes

1 S Woodland and others, *Repeat Study of Parents' Demand for Childcare*, Department for Education and Skills Research Report 348, 2002
2 HM Treasury, *Pre-Budget Report*, Cm 6042, 2003
3 L Harker, 'Childcare and Child Poverty', in P Dornan (ed) *Ending Child Poverty by 2020: the first three years*, Child Poverty Action Group, 2004
4 Department for Work and Pensions, *Opportunity For All*, Cm 5956, 2003
5 M Brewer and P Gregg, 'Lone Parents, the Working Families' Tax Credit and Employment in Households with Children', in *The State of Working Britain, Update 2001*, Centre for Economic Performance, 2001
6 Assuming a 10-year transition towards universal childcare: see M Ambler and others, *Costs and Benefits of Universal Childcare: a preliminary analysis for the UK*, PriceWaterhouseCoopers, 2003
7 E Melhuish, *A Literature Review of the Impact of Early Years Provision on Young Children, with Emphasis Given to Children from Disadvantaged Backgrounds*, for National Audit Office, 2004
8 P Gregg and E Washbrook, *The Effects of Early Maternal Employment on Child*

Development in the UK, CMPO Working Paper Series No 03/70, Bristol University, 2003

9 Department for Work and Pensions, *Opportunity For All*, Cm 5956, 2003

10 T Bertram and others, *Early Excellence Centre Pilot Programme Second Evaluation Report 2000-2001*, Department for Education and Skills Research Report 361, 2002

11 See M Ambler and others, *Costs and Benefits of Universal Childcare: a preliminary analysis for the UK*, PriceWaterhouseCoopers, 2003

12 TUC, *Response to the Childcare Review*, 2004

13 M Barnes and others, *Families and Children in Britain: findings from the 2002 Families and Children Study (FACS)*, Department for Work and Pensions Research Report 206, 2004

14 D Kasparova and others, *Families, Work and Childcare*, Department for Work and Pensions Research Report 191, 2003

15 See note 14

16 The DayCare Trust, *Facing the Childcare Challenge*, Briefing Paper, November 2003

17 Interchange 64, *Parents' Demand for Childcare in Scotland*, National Centre for Social Research, 2000

18 Inland Revenue, *Child and Working Tax Credits Quarterly Statistics*, April 2004

19 J Nicholls and C Simm, *The Childcare Tax Credit Element of Working Families' Tax Credit: a qualitative study*, MORI, Inland Revenue Research Report 7, 2003

20 HM Treasury, *Pre-Budget Report*, Cm 6042, 2003; see note 18

21 House of Commons *Hansard*, 28 February 2003, col 739w

22 See note 19

23 The DayCare Trust Press Notice quoting Ofsted figures, 2004

24 National Audit Office, *Early Years: progress in developing high quality childcare and early education accessible to all*, Session 2003/04, HC 268, 2004

25 T Harris and others, *Childcare: how local markets respond to national initiatives*, Department for Education and Skills Research Report 526, 2004

26 See note 14

27 See note 1

28 *Lone Parents and Childcare: the facts*, National Council for One Parent Families Briefing, June 2002

29 G Paull and others, *Mothers' Employment and Childcare Use in Britain*, Institute for Fiscal Studies, 2002

30 C Skinner, 'Childcare Provision', in J Bradshaw (ed), *The Well-being of Children in the UK*, Save the Children, 2002

31 See note 25

32 See for example, note 11
33 J Bradshaw and N Finch, *A Comparison of Child Benefit Packages in 22 Countries*, Department for Work and Pensions Research Report 174, 2002
34 Institute for Fiscal Studies, *Green Budget*, 2003
35 The average hourly amount spent on (a) informal and (b) formal childcare.
36 Taking an argument from M Brewer, *What do the Child Poverty Targets Mean for the Child Tax Credit? An update*, Institute for Fiscal Studies Briefing Note 41, 2003
37 TUC, *Response to the Childcare Review*, 2004
38 L Feinstein, 'Very Early Evidence', *CentrePiece* Summer 2003, Centre for Economic Performance, 2003

Summary and issues for the future

Summary

Child tax credit and child poverty

Child tax credit (CTC) is intended to offer support to all families, but also to be a mechanism to reduce child poverty (an example of 'progressive universalism'). Commentators have also suggested that recent increases in the per child element in CTC could help the Government meet its child income poverty targets (by 2004), all other things being equal. Its adequacy in meeting the needs of children depends on take-up being high and meeting more, if not all, of the costs of children in poorer families. We do not yet have enough evidence to say whether CTC is adequate in this respect.

Some possible future policy options include the following.

- Maintaining and improving the value of child benefit as the bedrock of support for most families with children.
- Ensuring that CTC continues to contribute towards reducing child income poverty by uprating the per child element so that it is regularly above earnings by substantial amounts.
- Considering ways to target additional help to poorer families with more than three children and where there is a child under five.
- Uprating the disabled child element to match the child element rises.
- Exploring the feasibility of making additional lump-sum 'child development credits' to children at key stages as a contribution towards meeting longer-term child poverty targets.

Assessing income and reporting changes

One of the features of the new tax credits is that awards are based on assessments of annual income, with provision to respond to income changes above £2,500 within the year.

Some possible policy options include the following.

- Making it clearer to recipients what changes they need to report and the consequences of not doing so. Award notices are often unclear and cover working tax credit (WTC) and CTC together. A clear statements could appear on an award notice saying that it should be kept until the final award notice for the year is received, as it will be needed to assist the process of renewing a claim.
- Considering if different rules for changes of circumstances would be appropriate for WTC and CTC if it seems that one is more affected by changes of circumstances than the other. For example, better-off families receiving the family element only might be more used to annual reporting but others, such as those receiving WTC and CTC, might encounter more frequent changes of circumstances.
- Examining whether a move to current year income assessments, basing awards on expected income (similar to the Australian system), would be more responsive to the needs of lower income families with children.
- Expanding the choice of payment options, such as:
  - making weekly payments of CTC where people are also on IS;
  - having a mix of regular and lump-sum payments;
  - allowing better-off families (ie, those in receipt of the family element only) to claim in advance of the tax year and receive a full year's payment, not just three months' backdating.

Being paid too much: overpayments

The stringent approach of the Inland Revenue to when overpayments occur and their recovery via deductions from tax credit payments (including where there has been an official error) have led to hardship in the first year of the scheme.

In summary, policy options could include the following.

- Making immediate changes to improve the administration of overpayments. This includes clearer award notices so that people know to what and the amount to which they are entitled, and what circumstances might alter their award. Overpayments should be notified separately, giving information about how they have arisen, the likely means of recovery and the additional top-up payments that can be made if hardship occurs.

- Ending in-year recovery of overpayments, as full recovery of an overpayment within the year can undermine child policy objectives. The Inland Revenue should consider taking recovery action only at the end of the year when full reconciliation is undertaken.
- Reducing the recovery rate of overpayments so that overpayments are collected more slowly, but leaving families with CTC payments that are only slightly below their entitlement. An alternative would be to pay top-up payments automatically.
- Ending the right to recover overpayments that have clearly resulted from official error and introducing statutory tests for recoverability.
- Reinstating the right to appeal a decision on tax credit overpayments and on whether they should be recovered.

Being paid too little: underpayments

Errors may occur in around one in ten tax credit claims, but in many cases the accuracy of awards will be unclear until the end of the year. People are not always clear what award they have been given. Effective estimates of take-up are not currently available, but full take-up of entitlement will be important in reducing child poverty.

Some policy options to reduce the likelihood of underpayments and to improve take-up include the following.

- Considering what may be needed to improve the quality of decision making and the number of errors.
- Extending backdating to 12 months where an award should have been made, or made at a higher rate, where this was a result of an official error.
- Revising award notices to make them clearer. This could include simple back-up leaflets explaining issues such as the right to appeal and to complain; how to read the award notice; what to do if the award looks wrong; rules about reporting changes; and how overpayments and underpayments can be dealt with.

- Emphasising the child poverty targets and the role of CTC in reducing child poverty in staff training and guidance.
- Developing a face-to-face service as well as a telephone service to increase take-up and improve the quality of the service.
- Publicising take-up estimates on a regular basis and undertaking partnerships with voluntary sector agencies to ensure that claims are made and processed quickly.
- Considering whether the level of compensation payments could mirror penalty amounts as an incentive to improve the quality of the service.
- Reviewing current IT arrangements with a view to improving the quality and speed of service for applicants.

Relationship with other benefits

The 'passporting' rules have become more complex with tax credits and people entitled to free school meals have not received them. The introduction of tax credits also highlights the needs for further reform to housing benefit (HB). Some short-term options include:

- Improving the notification of tax credits awards for passported benefits. This includes clearly identifying the different tax credit awards in the notice and referring to those passported benefits which could be claimed.
- Making entitlement to passported benefits automatic. Experience to date suggests that, because some passporting arrangements require people to make a separate claim, delays in entitlement to passported benefits can occur. This can be compounded if people do not have the correct award notice or cannot prove their tax credit entitlement. One option would be to make all passporting arrangements automatic. For example, the Inland Revenue could send notices to relevant authorities like local education authorities. Guidance to the relevant authorities that deal with passported benefits may also help.
- Simplifying the current passporting arrangements for health and education benefits, so that, for example, people could qualify for passported benefits if they are in receipt of CTC, except where only the family element is payable (better-off families). At the same time, to help the poorest families with children who may be on incomes only just above the income support (IS) level, allow people in receipt of the

maximum CTC to become eligible for discretionary social fund grants and loans for essential items at times of need.

- Tackling further HB anomalies, such as the income calculations and earnings disregards. Earnings disregards can be a particular problem where housing costs are high, leading to suggestions that a higher earnings disregard could apply in those areas (such as London) or some kind of 'London weighting' or disregard within WTC.

In the longer term the Government could consider a full or partial housing credit aligned with the new tax credits.

Childcare and child poverty

Childcare can make a significant contribution towards reducing child poverty by enabling parents to work, raising their incomes, and improving child development, which may help to reduce the risk that poor children will remain poor in adulthood. The number of childcare places has increased since 1997 but coverage remains patchy and costs are high. Help with some childcare costs can be met through the childcare tax credit, but as this is part of WTC it is tied to work status. There are longer-term issues about whether government support should be directed towards greater provision of (free or low-cost) formal childcare or helping parents to pay the market costs of existing provision.

Possible short-term policy options include the following.

- Extending the geographical coverage of children's centres. As almost half of poor families do not live in the 20 per cent most deprived areas chosen for children's centres, the Work and Pensions Select Committee recommended that these centres should be rolled out to the 30 per cent most deprived areas by 2006.
- Encouraging the development and use of formal (good quality) childcare, or at least increasing the proportion of formal care used. This could include prioritising expanding early years provision for children under three, which is often the most difficult to obtain and the most expensive. It may also, perhaps, be the most important from a child poverty perspective, as by age two damage to educational development may have been done: 60 per cent of children from low-income groups who perform less well on child development tests at that age

did not improve by age 10, and differences at 42 months strongly predict final educational qualifications.

In the longer term, there may be a case for having a package of greater availability of formal childcare and early years provision in all areas, available to all parents who want it, and which is either free or at reduced rate for low-income families. This could include a stand-alone childcare tax credit separate from WTC, meeting more of the costs of childcare for low-income families (whether in work or not).

Impact of the new tax credits: one year on

In the first year of CTC and WTC there is limited analysis to date from which to make a comprehensive assessment of the impact of the new tax credits. CPAG's experience thus far has been that the Government's agenda has reduced child poverty and, although most of the evidence on this predates CTC, there is good reason to suppose that this policy change will have further reduced the numbers of children in poverty. It is equally clear that there are shortcomings in the design of CTC that need to be reconsidered in the future.

Has child tax credit been portable between benefits and work?

There is limited evidence to date about the impact on moving in and out of work, and the final picture may not be clear until the people claiming IS and jobseeker's allowance (JSA) have been included in the tax credits system. Whilst in theory CTC can be claimed in and out of work, this can in some circumstances be compromised by the operation of recovering overpayments. Anecdotally, CPAG has heard of instances where people have left work as a result and where transitions in and out of work have not been speedily and accurately dealt with.

Has child tax credit worked to get payments for children to main carer?

Payments are generally made to the main carer and by the end of the first year almost 88 per cent of CTC awards were paid to women. However, there is limited evidence to date about the extent to which this transfer of payment, and other features of CTC, has made it a more transparent payment for the needs of children. This too may not be clear until the separation of child and adult payments has been completed for people on IS and JSA.

Is it a more transparent, streamlined system which brings all income-related payments into a single credit?

Transparency in the sense of understanding entitlement can be clouded by complexity. This is probably one of the major design problems for the new tax credits. It is probably easier to calculate what someone might receive in theory than to relate it to actual circumstances. As noted in Chapters 3 and 4, rules about which year's income counts, adjustments made to awards during the year and the way overpayments are handled make it more difficult for individuals to understand entitlement. Transparency may also be clouded by the provisional nature of payments until the end of the year. Those in the least transparent part of the system (ie, those entitled to maximum awards) are most likely to be the poorest. Passported benefits probably add to the lack of transparency. In contrast, better-off families with just the family element have less complexity to deal with and so may find the system more straightforward.

How has a common framework for assessment and payment, so all families are included in the same system, operated?

The family element, payable to most families, is fundamental to the aim of ensuring that CTC is a single, inclusive system of supporting families. However, as this element has not been uprated its value will be reduced relative to poorer families. This may be appropriate as a means of reducing child poverty but it also suggests that there are limits to 'progressive universalism'. The use of tax rules for some issues like overpayments and penalties may be more familiar to better-off families but can have punitive effects on low-income families. Indeed, the Inland Revenue 'culture' may still be more focussed on people who owe money rather than people who need to claim in order to avoid falling into income poverty.

Future policy options

Short-term options

Some of the options discussed above could be achieved within a short period, such as improving the administration (through clearer award notices, ensuring that people know what circumstances to report and when) and making some small-scale changes to parts of the system that impact significantly on poorer families (such as overpayment recovery rates, improved passporting and limited changes to HB).

Longer-term options and child poverty

Although the Government may be on track to meet its 2004/05 child poverty targets, more needs to be done to meet the longer-term targets. Both CTC and an extended supply of affordable childcare will be crucial to longer-term success. In particular, CTC will need to be delivered more efficiently and responsively to meet the needs of the poorest families. As an important mechanism to reduce child income poverty, having a longer-term commitment to uprating CTC in line with and above average earnings will be important as we move towards the next phase of child poverty targets (2010 and 2020). Child benefit is also important and its value also needs to be maintained and improved.

Other longer-term options include developing a better balance between the provision of childcare and support to meet the costs, as well as the range of options for a housing credit.

Appendix one
Rules for reporting changes in circumstances

Changes in circumstances that must be reported

The following changes must be notified within three months.[1]

- The claimant either stops being part of the couple who made a joint claim or stops being a single claimant. In these circumstances, tax credit entitlement comes to an end from the time the change occurred and the claimant must make a new claim.
- The claimant leaves the UK permanently, or for more than eight weeks (12 weeks if the reason for leaving is because the claimant was ill, or a member of her/his family was ill or has died). Again, in these circumstances tax credit entitlement comes to an end and the claimant must make a new claim.
- Weekly childcare costs either cease or reduce by £10 a week or more for four weeks in a row. The change in entitlement takes effect from the first day of the week following the four weeks in a row in which the change occurred.
- The claimant loses the right to reside in the UK.

If someone fails to report one of these changes within three months they might incur a financial penalty.

Changes in circumstances that are optional to report

It is optional to report changes during the year that affect maximum entitlement to child tax credit (CTC) – ie, one of the elements. They can be notified at the end of the year when the end-of-year reconciliation takes place. However, it is usually desirable to report the change as soon as possible. Changes that *increase* entitlement can only be backdated for three months from the date of notifying the Inland Revenue. Changes that *decrease* entitlement take effect from the date of the change, so an overpayment can occur if notification is delayed.

The sort of changes these rules apply to include:[2]

- having a new baby or if another child joins the family;
- if a child leaves the family to live with someone else;
- if a child starts or stops full-time education after 1 September following her/his 16th birthday;
- if a claimant changes her/his employer or the number of hours s/he works;
- if childcare costs increase by £10 or more a week for at least four weeks in a row.

Changes in income[3]

The initial decision is usually based on the previous tax year's income. The award can be changed to reflect:

- any expected fall in annual income compared with that used to make the initial decision (for example, where earnings fall during the year);
- any expected rise in income compared with that used to make the initial decision, where that rise is more than £2,500 a year.

It is optional to report changes in income. These are taken into account at the end of the tax year, but it might be desirable to report them earlier so as to avoid an overpayment or underpayment.

Renewal awards[4]

At the end of the tax year, the Inland Revenue finalises the previous year's award and, if appropriate, sets up an award for the current year. This may be known as the 'end-of-year reconciliation' or, alternatively, 'annual review'. Claimants receive an annual review form detailing the circumstances on which the previous year's award was based. For around a third of claimants – those getting only the family element of CTC – there is no need to contact the Inland Revenue provided their income for the previous year is within the range given on the annual review form and there is no change in household circumstances. The remaining two-thirds of claimants must complete an annual declaration form giving details of income for the year just passed. This must be returned by 30 September otherwise the award stops. It resumes once people provide the required information and, so long as this is before the end of January and there is good cause for the delay, the award is fully backdated. Self-employed people and others who are able to give only an estimate of the previous year's income by the end of September must provide details of actual income by the end of January. Failing to meet deadlines can result in financial penalties.

Notes

1 *Welfare Benefits and Tax Credits Handbook, 2004/05*, Child Poverty Action Group, p1382
2 See note 1, p1383
3 See note 1, p1384
4 See note 1, p1369

Appendix two
Overpayments and penalties

When an overpayment can occur[1]

The most likely circumstances in which an overpayment can occur are when:

- income rose by more than £2,500 in the tax year and (intentionally or not) the claimant did not tell the Inland Revenue;
- the claimant did not tell the Inland Revenue in time about a change of circumstances reducing her/his entitlement (see Appendix 1);
- the information the claimant gave to the Inland Revenue was incorrect;
- none of the above apply, but an overpayment occurred anyway because of an official error.

Overpayments during the year of the award

Decisions on whether an overpayment has occurred can be made during the year in the following circumstances.

- If the Inland Revenue thinks there is likely to be an overpayment, it can amend the award (or an award of another tax credit) in order to reduce or wipe out the overpayment. This can mean that the award is reduced for the rest of the year. If the Inland Revenue thinks a claimant has already been paid all the tax credits to which s/he is likely to be entitled for the whole year, it may stop paying altogether. However, it cannot take any of this action once a final decision on entitlement for the year has been made.
- If an award is terminated on the grounds that a claimant did not satisfy the basic conditions of entitlement, the Inland Revenue may decide

that the amount already paid (or some of it) is to be regarded as an overpayment. The basic conditions for child tax credit are that a person is responsible for a child and for working tax credit that a person is regarded as being in full-time work.

Overpayments at or after the end of the award

The Inland Revenue can also decide that an overpayment has occurred at or after the end of the tax year concerned, when it may make any of the following decisions:

- final decision;
- enquiry decision;
- decision on discovery;
- revision for official error.

The Inland Revenue recovers the overpayment most commonly from the following year's award at fixed rates. It has the discretion to waive all or part of the overpayment if recovery would cause hardship or if the overpayment arose through official error and the claimant could reasonably have thought that her/his award was correct.

Financial penalties[2]

The Inland Revenue can impose a financial penalty where someone has failed to comply with requirements in the following circumstances:

- fraudulently or negligently making an incorrect statement or declaration, or supplying incorrect information or evidence;
- failing to provide information or evidence for a decision on an initial claim, during the course of an award, a revision during an award, a final decision, or an enquiry;
- failing to comply with a requirement regarding a final notice (ie, annual review or annual declaration form);
- failing to notify a specified change of circumstances – ie:

- a decrease of £10 a week or more over four weeks in a row in childcare costs;
- the claimant has stopped claiming as a single claimant;
- the claimant was claiming as a couple but is no longer part of that couple. This includes if the claimant or her/his partner leave the UK permanently or go abroad for more than a set time.

Maximum penalties

The maximum penalty for incorrect statements and information is £3,000, and for failure to comply, £300 (if concerning failure to provide information, there is a further daily penalty of up to £60 a day until the information is provided). In both cases penalties have to be paid 30 days after notification.

The Inland Revenue has the discretion to impose a penalty and the amount. If an agreement cannot be made, the Inland Revenue has a legal power of recovery.

Notes

1 *Welfare Benefits and Tax Credits Handbook 2004/05*, Child Poverty Action Group, 2004, p1388
2 See note 1, p1400

Appendix three
Childcare tax credit eligibility

Who is eligible?

To qualify for the childcare element of working tax credit (WTC) someone has to be either a lone parent in work or a couple where one or both are in work, or one is in work and the other 'incapacitated' (receiving incapacity or disability benefit).

From April 2004, other changes extend help with childcare costs.

- First-time parents who were working at least 16 hours a week before going on maternity, paternity or adoption leave are able to claim WTC from the date of birth or adoption of their first child.
- Mothers on paid maternity leave are able to receive help with the costs of childcare for their new babies. This rule is necessary because the childcare element is part of WTC and maternity leave only counts for the purposes of WTC if someone was in full-time work before she went on leave (someone without a child would have to be working for 30 hours before s/he qualified, so this is particularly important for first-time mothers).

What type of childcare is eligible?

Parents can claim support for the costs of using approved childcare. This includes:

- childcare provided by a registered childminder or other registered providers (nurseries, after-school clubs, local authority day services);
- schools or other establishments exempt from registration;
- out-of-hours clubs on school premises;

- childcare schemes run by approved providers for children aged seven or more (for example, breakfast clubs, holiday play schemes);
- a child carer who is approved to care for children in the parents' home (in England only);
- a domiciliary worker or nurse from a registered agency caring for children in the parents' home (in England only).

The 2003 *Pre-Budget Report* announced that in Spring 2004, the Government would be consulting on streamlining the process of registration and how to widen 'home childcare'. Following a review in early 2003, the Government also announced new measures to encourage employer-supported childcare. From April 2005:

- tax exemption will be extended to cover formal registered childcare or approved home childcare contracted by the employer (such as a childminder);
- the requirement for the employer to have management responsibility for the childcare provision will be removed;
- there will be a new matching tax exemption for childcare vouchers;
- schemes will be accessible to all employees.[1]

The tax and national insurance exemption will be restricted to approved childcare and limited to £50 a week per employee (to ensure that the exemption is affordable and targeted). The Institute for Fiscal Studies commented that fewer than 60,000 employees currently take advantage of schemes such as workplace nurseries and vouchers, and some low-income parents would instead be better off by taking a higher wage and then claiming the childcare tax credit.[2]

From June 2004 parents using breakfast clubs run by schools and those paying for childcare provided by foster carers will be eligible for the childcare element of WTC, and a new 'light-touch' voluntary accreditation scheme to expand the range of eligible childcare is being considered.

Responding to changes in childcare

Since April 2003 there have been new rules to cover short-term changes in childcare. Parents who pay amounts that vary during the course of a year (such as those who only use childcare during school holidays) can work out an average across the whole year. If childcare costs reduce by more than £10 a week for four or more weeks in a row, the Inland Revenue must be notified – otherwise a penalty of £300 could be incurred. Rather than getting written confirmation of their childcare arrangements from the provider, the claimant now only has to keep a record of the childcare costs and childminders will only be asked to respond to a simple check in a percentage of cases to confirm that a child is in their care.[3]

There may be further changes to the way childcare costs are calculated (see CPAG's *Welfare Rights Bulletins* for updates).

Other help with childcare costs

Other help includes the housing benefit and council tax benefit disregard against earnings for childcare costs. In 2003 these were £94.50 for one child and £140 for two or more children. These disregards have since been increased by 40 per cent to the WTC levels, with further possibilities of alignment also being considered (see Chapter 5). However, this appears to operate as a flat-rate maximum rather than 70 per cent of the maximum, as with WTC.[4] For people receiving non-means-tested benefits, some childcare costs can be deducted from earnings, but this is calculated differently from the WTC.

Notes

1 HM Treasury, *Pre-Budget Report*, Cm 6042, 2003
2 Institute for Fiscal Studies Press Release, 10 December 2003
3 Inland Revenue, *The New Tax Credits: a regulatory impact assessment*, 2001
4 S Osborne, 'Forthcoming Attractions: children and childcare', *Welfare Rights Bulletin*, February 2004